Animals!
Animals!

What They Are, What They Do

I WONDER

Science begins with
wondering. What do
you wonder about when you
see animals like the ones
shown here?

Work with a partner to make
a list of questions you may
have about animals. Be ready
to share your list with the rest
of the class.

◄ **Raccoon family at a pond**

▼ **Yellow-billed magpie family**

I PLAN

You may have asked questions such as these as you wondered about animals. Scientists also ask questions. Then they plan ways to help them find answers to their questions. Now you and your classmates can plan how you will investigate animals.

My Science Log

- Why are animals different from one another?

- In what ways are animals grouped?

- How do animals protect themselves?

- Why do some birds fly south for the winter?

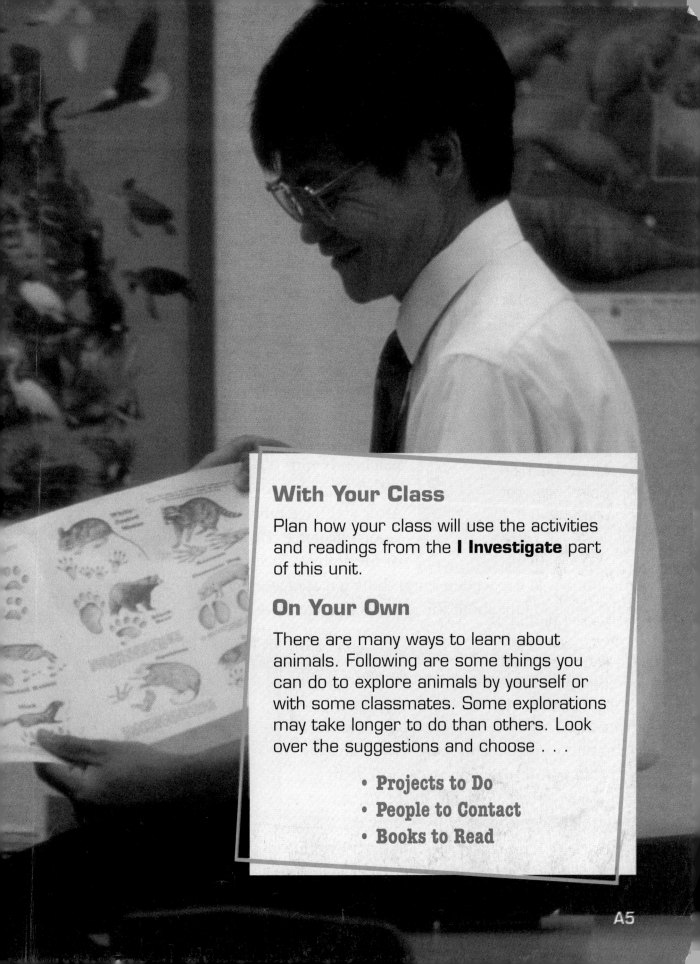

With Your Class

Plan how your class will use the activities and readings from the **I Investigate** part of this unit.

On Your Own

There are many ways to learn about animals. Following are some things you can do to explore animals by yourself or with some classmates. Some explorations may take longer to do than others. Look over the suggestions and choose . . .

- **Projects to Do**
- **People to Contact**
- **Books to Read**

PROJECTS TO DO

ANIMAL TRACKER

Animals leave clues behind that tell you they were there. Each type of animal has its own type of track. Look for animal tracks in mud, sand, or snow. You can also leave a pan of sand outside at night and look for tracks in it in the morning. Speak with someone who knows about animals, or use books in the library, to identify the animals that made the tracks.

SCIENCE FAIR PROJECT

Design and make an animal feeder. Your feeder could be either for birds or for squirrels. Discuss your ideas with your teacher. If your teacher approves, collect your materials. Then build your feeder. After you have built your feeder, observe it from a distance. Do not try to touch any of the animals. Instead, take notes about the animals at the feeder. Then show a classmate your feeder and use your notes to talk about the animals that eat from it.

ANIMAL RESEARCHER

There are many kinds of animals all over the world. Choose one to learn more about. You could observe one outside in your backyard or in a nearby park. Or you might watch a nature show on television, read a magazine, or use books from the library. Where does your animal live? How does the

animal find food, water, and shelter? Write three paragraphs about your animal. Share your paragraphs with a family member.

PEOPLE TO CONTACT

IN PERSON

Talk to a forest ranger at a state or national park or an animal specialist at a wildlife park. Ask about the animals that live there. Find out what the animals need to live. Design and write a booklet that other students can read to learn about the animals in the park.

- The Cousteau Society
- National Audubon Society
- National Park Service
- National Wildlife Federation
- U.S. Fish and Wildlife Service
- World Wildlife Fund

BY MAIL

Many government agencies and private groups study animals and help protect them. You can write to them for information. Here is a list of agencies and groups that you might try. Make a poster to share what you find out.

BY COMPUTER

Perhaps the computers at your school are connected to NGS Kids Network. That's an electronic network for students that was started by the National Geographic Society. You may be able to use the NGS Kids Network to find out more about animals around the world. Ask students in other countries what kinds of animals live near them. Also ask what kinds of pets are common. Write a report that tells something about the animal you thought was the most interesting. Read your report to the rest of the class.

BOOKS TO READ

How the Guinea Fowl Got Her Spots

by Barbara Knutson (Carolrhoda, 1990). This is a story of two friends, a little bird called a *guinea fowl* and a big cow. They have an enemy, a fierce lion. In this book, you'll find out how the little bird saves her friend from the hungry lion. You'll also discover how the cow helps the guinea fowl change the way she looks so she can hide from her enemies.

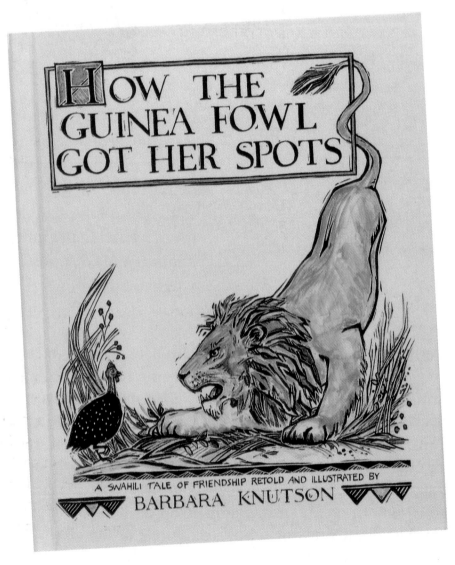

One Earth, a Multitude of Creatures

by Peter Roop and Connie Roop (Walker, 1992), Outstanding Science Trade Book. In this book, you'll spend 24 hours with many different animals that live in the Pacific Northwest. A bear takes honey from bees while other bears catch trout to eat. A trout snaps at an insect. A caterpillar chews leaves, and a bird snatches the caterpillar. You'll find out how all animals depend on each other and on the world around them.

One Earth, a Multitude of Creatures

PETER AND CONNIE ROOP
ILLUSTRATIONS BY VALERIE A. KELLS

More Books to Read

Animals Don't Wear Pajamas

by Eve B. Feldman (Henry Holt, 1992), Outstanding Science Trade Book. Animals need sleep, but they don't have beds and pillows or pajamas as we do. Some sleep at night, and others sleep in the daytime. This book will tell you about some ways animals sleep.

Busy Busy Squirrels

by Colleen Stanley Bare (Cobblehill Books, 1991), Outstanding Science Trade Book. If you were a squirrel, what would you do all day? You would carry food in pouches in your cheeks. You would hide from owls and other predators. You would do many things to find food and to stay safe. Squirrels are busy!

Where Are My Swans, Whooping Cranes, and Singing Loons?

by Ron Hirschi (Bantam Books, 1992). This book has exciting photos of birds and of the places where they live. Unfortunately, something is destroying the wetlands where these birds live. When birds lose their homes, they also lose their food and the places where they raise their young. Read about what is causing this problem and about what can be done to help solve it.

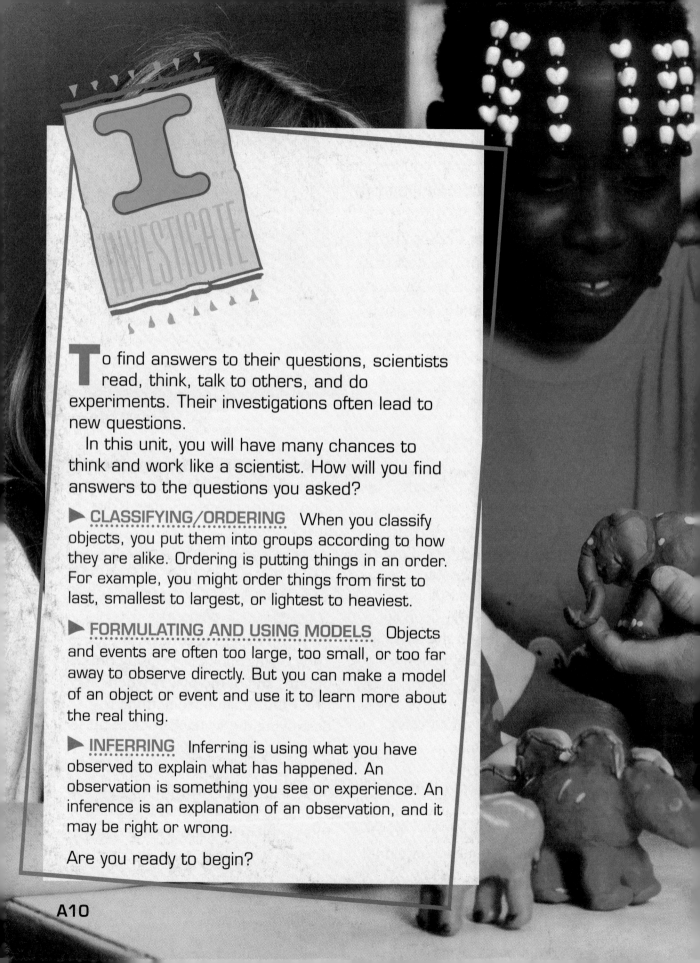

I INVESTIGATE

To find answers to their questions, scientists read, think, talk to others, and do experiments. Their investigations often lead to new questions.

In this unit, you will have many chances to think and work like a scientist. How will you find answers to the questions you asked?

▶ CLASSIFYING/ORDERING When you classify objects, you put them into groups according to how they are alike. Ordering is putting things in an order. For example, you might order things from first to last, smallest to largest, or lightest to heaviest.

▶ FORMULATING AND USING MODELS Objects and events are often too large, too small, or too far away to observe directly. But you can make a model of an object or event and use it to learn more about the real thing.

▶ INFERRING Inferring is using what you have observed to explain what has happened. An observation is something you see or experience. An inference is an explanation of an observation, and it may be right or wrong.

Are you ready to begin?

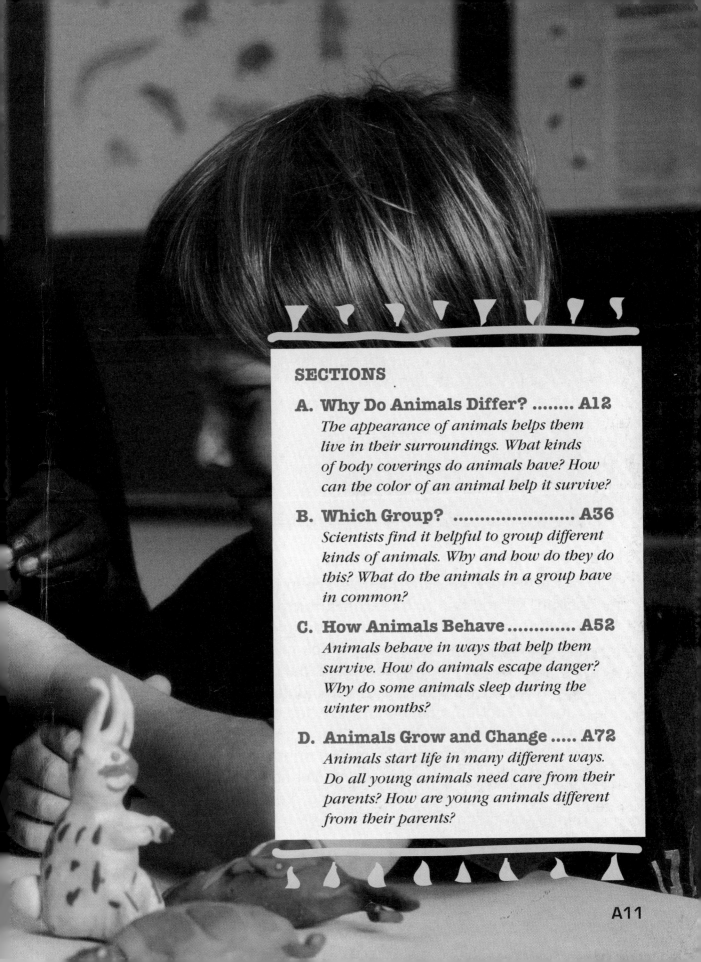

SECTIONS

Why Do Animals Differ?

Everywhere outside animals are in action. Wings flap and feathers flutter at a bird feeder. A cat sees the birds and slowly creeps toward them. A huge black crow chases away five little birds. A fat green lizard darts into the bushes, safe from harm. There are many kinds of animals.

In this section, you'll find out what animals need in order to live. You'll also learn about the features that make animals different from one another. Why do animals differ in so many ways? What features help them survive? In your Science Log, keep a record of the things you discover about animals.

1 WHAT DO ANIMALS NEED?

Have you ever seen a dog that wanted to let its owner know it was hungry? Some dogs sit quietly in front of their bowls and wait. Others bark and scratch at the cabinet where their food is kept. Whatever the animal does, it is letting its owner know about one of its needs.

Food is not the only thing a dog needs. It also needs water, air, and shelter. In fact, all animals need these things.

Animals need energy in order to move. An animal's body produces energy from food. The kind of food it needs depends on the animal. For example, sheep eat grass, and lions eat other animals.

▲ These beagles are eating the food they need to survive.

These llamas are eating the type of food they need. ▼

A healthful diet for people is made up of many different kinds of food. The food pyramid in the picture shows what a healthful diet consists of for a person.

Milk, yogurt, cheese

Fats, oils, sweets

The food pyramid shows the kinds of food you need to eat to stay healthy. ▶

Meat, poultry, fish, dry beans, eggs, nuts

Vegetables

Fruits

Breads, cereal, rice, pasta

Some animals get all the water they need from their bodily functions or from the food they eat. But most animals must drink water to survive.

The kangaroo rat lives in the desert areas of the southwest United States and Mexico. Its water comes from its own body processes. ▶

These warthogs are drinking from a watering hole. ▼

Put your hand on your chest. Do you notice that it moves up and down? That's because you're breathing in and out all the time. When you breathe, you take in a gas called *oxygen*, which you need in order to live. All animals that live on land get their oxygen from the air.

A sperm whale can stay underwater for up to 75 minutes. But then it must come to the water's surface to breathe air. Many other animals that live in water must come to the surface to breathe.

Animals must protect themselves from enemies and from the weather. A shelter helps keep an animal safe, dry, and warm or cool.

Many animals build their own shelters. Birds build nests. Prairie dogs dig deep tunnels for their burrows. Beavers build their lodges by making tall piles of sticks and branches in streams.

▲ This humpback whale needs air to live.

This bird has made a nest in a tree. ▼

LESSON 1 REVIEW

❶ You have the same needs that other animals have—for food, water, air, and shelter. How do you meet those needs?

❷ Suppose you were given a rabbit to care for. What would you do to make sure it survived?

A15

2 BODY COVERINGS

You've just read that all animals have the same basic needs. But not all animals are alike. One way that animals differ from one another is in their body coverings. Each type of body covering helps the animal in some way.

Scales and Feathers

Some animals, such as fish, are covered with scales. Birds are covered with feathers. How do these body coverings help animals survive?

What do a fish's scales do? Fish have scales that are a part of the skin and cover the body. Scales lie in neat rows. They overlap, just like shingles on a roof. And like a roof, they protect what's underneath. Scales help protect the fish from other animals that live in the water and from some types of disease.

▲ This is a white perch. You can see its scales.

▲ This is a close-up of the white perch's scales. You can see how they overlap.

Fish are not the only animals covered with scales. Lizards have scales, too. A lizard's scales help keep its body from drying out. What other animals have scales?

Have you ever seen a newborn chick? It looks soft and cuddly because it has a layer of fluffy down feathers. Like a warm sweater, *down feathers* help keep the young bird warm. Down feathers trap heat from the bird's body and hold the heat close to its skin.

When a bird gets older, *contour feathers* cover the down. Contour feathers are a little like scales. They overlap and help keep a bird from getting soaked in the rain. The waterproof covering of contour feathers on top of down is like a jacket on top of a sweater. Down feathers trap the heat, and contour feathers keep the down feathers dry.

This nene (NAY nay) goose has different layers of feathers. ▼

▲ This is a down feather. The edges of the feather do not lock together. Instead, they spread out and help trap air. This air stays next to the bird's body and keeps it warm.

◄ This contour feather is different from a down feather. The small parts of a contour feather are hooked together, forming a stiff, flat surface.

THINK ABOUT IT

1. Explain why scales are important.

2. How do contour feathers help keep birds dry?

ACTIVITY

How Does Fur Help Animals?

How can you find out for yourself how fur helps an animal? You can make a model of an animal with fur. In this activity, you'll use two cans of water instead of animals. And you'll use cotton instead of fur.

DO THIS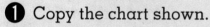

1 Copy the chart shown.

2 **CAUTION: Watch out for the edges on the cans.**
Take the paper off both cans.

MATERIALS

- 2 empty soup cans
- white glue
- cotton
- hot water
- 2 thermometers
- stopwatch
- Science Log data sheet

HOW COTTON AFFECTS WATER TEMPERATURE		
Time	Water Temperature in Can With Cotton	Water Temperature in Can Without Cotton

3 Spread glue around the outside of one can. Then put a thick layer of cotton around the can. Wait for the glue to dry, and then fluff the cotton.

A18

4 **CAUTION: Be careful with the hot water.** Your teacher will fill both cans with hot water.

5 Place a thermometer in each can, and record the temperature of the water. The temperatures in the cans should be about the same at first. Record the time.

6 Check the temperature of the water in each can every 10 minutes for 30 minutes. Record the temperatures in the chart.

THINK AND WRITE

1. In which can did the water stay hot longer? Why?

2. Think about the clothes that people wear. How are some clothes like the thick fur on a bear?

3. FORMULATING AND USING MODELS Many times you cannot observe an object directly. So you might make a model, instead. In this activity, you made a model of an animal with fur. Why was using a model easier than observing an animal?

Fur

In the activity, you discovered how fur helps keep animals warm. Like down feathers, fur holds body heat next to the animal's skin.

During the winter months, some animals' coats of fur become longer and thicker. When an animal is very cold, it fluffs up its fur. Muscles in the skin make each hair in the fur stand up.

Your own skin does the same thing. When you feel cold, you may get goose bumps. These small bumps all over your skin make your body hair stand up. Next time you have goose bumps, see if you can find a tiny hair at the center of each bump.

▲ You can see the fur on this kangaroo. Fur protects the kangaroo's skin and keeps the kangaroo warm.

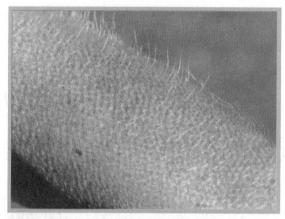

▲ This is what goose bumps look like close up.

Scales, feathers, and fur all help protect animals. These body coverings are adaptations (ad uhp TAY shuhnz). An **adaptation** is any body covering, body part, or behavior that helps an animal live in its environment.

QUICK CHECK

LESSON 2 REVIEW

❶ How do adaptations such as scales, feathers, and fur help animals?

❷ If you put on a coat before you go outside, you'll stay warm. But if you put it on after you're cold, the coat doesn't help you to feel warm right away. Why?

3 HOW ANIMALS HIDE

As you found out earlier, animals need food. What kinds of foods do animals eat? Where do they get their food? You'll have a chance to find out in the following investigations.

Predator or Prey?

If you're hungry, what do you do? You probably walk into the kitchen and find something to eat. Or perhaps you and your family go to the grocery store. Animals can't go to the grocery store. How do they find food?

In the wild, there aren't any kitchens or grocery stores for animals. So animals spend a lot of their time trying to find something to eat. The way they do this depends on the animals and their needs.

Some animals eat only plants. Other animals eat plants and other small animals. Some animals eat only other animals. An animal that catches and eats other animals is called a **predator. Prey** is any animal that may become food for another animal. For example, lions are predators that eat antelopes. Antelopes often become lions' prey.

▲ There are two animals in this picture. Which animal is the predator? Which animal is the prey?

THINK ABOUT IT
What is the difference between predator and prey?

A21

ACTIVITY

How Color Helps

Animals come in all different colors. Some animals, such as parrots, are bright and flashy. Other animals, such as toads, are plain brown or green. Find out how color might help keep an animal safe. In this activity, think of yourself as a hungry bird looking for worms and insects hiding in the grass.

DO THIS

❶ Copy this chart.

FINDING TOOTHPICKS	
Color	Number Found

MATERIALS

- colored toothpicks
- stopwatch
- small brown paper bag
- Science Log data sheet

❷ In this activity, you'll be a predator. The prey you'll hunt for will be colored toothpicks.

❸ Your teacher will scatter the toothpicks on a grassy area.

❹ When your teacher says "Hunt," pick up as many toothpick "animals" as you can in 30 seconds. Keep your captured prey in the bag.

❺ Count the toothpicks that you find of each color. Record your results in the chart.

❻ What color did you find most often? What color did you find least often? Compare your results with your classmates' results.

THINK AND WRITE

1. Think about the colors that were the hardest to find. How do those colors compare with the color of the grass?

2. Explain how an insect's color helps it survive.

Camouflage

You've just discovered how an animal's color can make the animal hard to see. How would this help the animal survive?

The adaptation that allows animals to blend into their surroundings is known as **camouflage** (KAM uh flahzh). An animal's surroundings are also called its **habitat**. Every animal has a habitat. A chimpanzee's habitat is a jungle. A trout's habitat is a freshwater stream.

In some cold areas, the colors of an animal's habitat change during the year. Think about brown soil, green leaves, and green grass. In the winter, leaves drop from trees, and snow hides the grass and soil. How can an animal match its habitat all year? Some animals, such as the snowshoe hare, have fur that changes color when the weather turns cold.

◄ In the summer, the snowshoe hare is brown.

In the winter, a thick coat of white fur covers the hare's body. ▶

Color is not the only adaptation that helps camouflage an animal. Some animals can hide because of the patterns on their body coverings. The tiger's stripes help it hide in dry grasses. In this way, the tiger can watch its prey without being seen. When the time is right, the tiger will run and pounce on its prey.

◀ How does camouflage help this Bengal tiger?

Other animals are hidden by their body shape. The walking stick is an insect shaped like a twig. It is camouflaged by its shape, color, and pattern.

Why do you think this insect is called a walking stick? ▶

THINK ABOUT IT

Explain how camouflage helps both predators and prey.

A24

Hide-and-Seek

Some animals can run, swim, or fly away to escape predators. But what about animals that can't do this? Many of them hide. Some hide right out in the open! Find out how an animal's adaptive coloring and shape help it survive. Try to find the animal camouflaged in each of these pictures.

▲ Find the flounder. This fish lies very still at the bottom of the bay.

Find the leaf katydid. ▼

▲ How many snake pipefish can you find? How do you think these fish got their name?

▲ Find the horned frog.

QUICK CHECK

LESSON 3 REVIEW

Suppose you've been asked to camouflage a pencil and to put it somewhere in your classroom. How would you camouflage the pencil? What materials would you use? How is a camouflaged pencil like a camouflaged animal?

A25

4 SUITED TO THEIR FOOD

Your stomach is making funny noises, and you feel tired. What's wrong? You're hungry! Like other animals, you need to eat. Food gives you energy and helps you grow. Your body is adapted so that you can eat many foods. Find out how animals are adapted to eat their foods.

ACTIVITY

How Do Beaks Help Birds?

Birds have different types of beaks that help them eat the foods they need. Suppose that the tools in this activity are different beaks. Find the tool that works best for picking up and "eating" each type of food.

DO THIS

1 Make a chart like the one below.

MATERIALS

- chopsticks
- drinking straw
- pliers
- clothespin
- spoon
- tweezers
- plastic worms
- cooked spaghetti
- rice
- raisins
- birdseed
- peanuts in shells
- water in a paper cup
- Science Log data sheet

BIRD FOOD AND BEAK OBSERVATIONS		
Food	Best Tool (Beak)	Observations
Plastic worms		
Spaghetti		
Rice		
Raisins		
Birdseed		
Peanuts		
Water		

2 Put the chopsticks, straw, pliers, clothespin, spoon, and tweezers on one side of a desk. Think of these tools as beaks of different shapes. For example, you might think of the pliers as a beak that is short and thick.

3 Put all the rest of the materials on the other side of the desk. Think of them as bird food.

4 Put one type of food in the middle of the desk. Try picking up the food with each type of beak. Which beak is best for picking up the food? Which beak is best for crushing the food? Record your observations in the chart.

5 Test all the other foods, one at a time, in the same way.

THINK AND WRITE

Study your chart. Which kind of beak is best for picking up insects? for crushing birdseed? for digging up worms? for sipping water?

A JOURNEY to Discovery

More than 150 years ago, a scientist named Charles Darwin took an amazing trip. On that trip he discovered the same thing you did in the activity. He learned that birds' beaks are like tools that are suited to different jobs. Read on to find out more about his journey.

◄ Charles Darwin

At the age of 22, Charles Darwin left England on a five-year trip. He planned to study the different kinds of plants and animals around the world. In September of 1835, Darwin's ship landed at one of the Galápagos (guh LAH puh gohs) Islands in the Pacific Ocean. Darwin explored 15 of the islands and observed the plants and animals. He saw many small birds called *finches*.

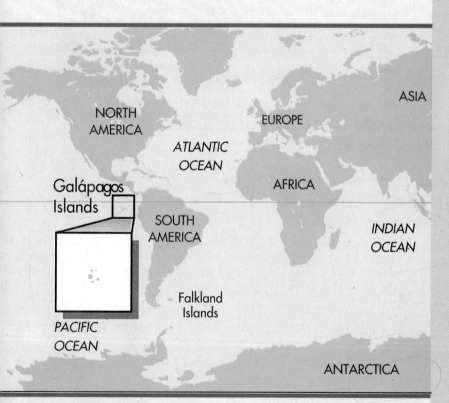

▲ The Galápagos Islands are in the Pacific Ocean.

Darwin observed that the finches on the islands looked very much alike, except for one thing. Their beaks were different in size and shape.

He also observed that the finches ate different kinds of food. Some ate seeds. Others ate fruit or insects. One kind of finch used a tool to help it eat. It held a small stick in its beak to dig insects from under tree bark.

Darwin recorded his observations in a notebook. He wondered why birds that looked so much alike had differently shaped beaks.

When he returned to England, he thought about what he had observed. More than 20 years later, he wrote a book about his ideas. In his book, Darwin explained how both plants and animals have changed over thousands of years.

This finch holds a cactus spine in its beak. Then it uses the spine to pick out insects from the cracks in the bark. ▼

◀ This finch has a sharp, pointed beak. It eats insects.

What did Charles Darwin learn about the finches? He discovered that over time, the beaks became adapted to the kind of food the bird ate. His ideas changed the ways people thought about animals. 📖

◀ This finch eats big seeds. It uses its heavy beak to crack them open.

▲ This finch has a curved beak. It eats buds and leaves.

THINK ABOUT IT

Explain why the beaks of the Galápagos finches have different shapes.

Animal Teeth

Birds aren't the only animals adapted to their foods. Some animals have teeth that are useful for just the foods they eat. For example, many animals that hunt have sharp, pointed teeth for eating meat. These teeth stab and slice.

Other animals have sharp, flat-edged teeth that cut like scissors. These teeth can clip grass and other plants. Wide, flat teeth are good for grinding food—especially plants.

Some animals have teeth that are useful for only a few types of food. How do the horse's teeth help it eat grass? ▶

Horse

Lion

◀ Look at the size and shape of this lion's teeth. What kinds of food do you think it eats?

People can eat all kinds of food—from peanut butter to apples to meat. How do your teeth help you eat both plants and meat? ▼

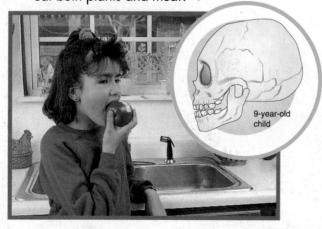

9-year-old child

QUICK CHECK

LESSON 4 REVIEW

How are birds' beaks and animals' teeth the same? How are they different? Write a short paragraph to explain.

5 UNIQUE ANIMALS

You've seen some of the ways an animal is adapted to its habitat. A fox's fur coat gets extra thick in the winter. Some animals have colors and shapes that camouflage them. Birds' beaks and animals' teeth are adapted for their food.

Animals Around the World

Here are pictures of animals from around the world. Read to find out how each animal's adaptations help it survive in its habitat.

Penguins are one type of bird that lives in Antarctica. Penguins are different from most other birds because they can't fly. But they're good at swimming and at keeping warm in very cold places. Penguins are covered with short feathers that make a waterproof covering for their body. Their sleek bodies, flipper-like wings, and webbed feet help them move through the water.

An emperor penguin swimming ▼

Snakes can be found almost anywhere that's not too cold. Pit vipers are snakes that live in North and South America. A bite from a pit viper can be deadly. Its bite helps the snake catch prey and protect itself from predators. Pit vipers also have another interesting adaptation. Pits, or small holes, near their eyes can sense heat. The pits help vipers find food and stay out of danger, even in the dark.

▲ A Pacific rattlesnake is a type of pit viper.

Camels are adapted to live in hot, dry deserts, such as those found in Asia. A camel can go for as long as 17 days without drinking water. A camel's nose can close to keep out blowing desert sand. Its thick eyebrows keep the sun out of its eyes.

▲ A Bactrian camel

◀ African elephants

African elephants are the largest animals that live on land. You might notice their large ears and trunks. Heat escapes through their ears, keeping the animals cool. They can use their trunks to reach for food, to smell, to drink, and to blow dust on themselves. The dust covers their skin and keeps it from burning in the hot sun.

THINK ABOUT IT

Why do animals have so many different adaptations?

What Can an Armadillo Do?

You've learned about many kinds of adaptations. Now read about a very unusual animal. See if you can figure out what its adaptations are.

It's an Armadillo!

by **Bianca Lavies**
from *It's an Armadillo!*

LITERATURE What has left these tracks in the sand? Something with four feet and a tail. You can see its footprints. You can see the groove made by its tail. Where did it go?

Into its burrow underground. The burrow keeps it cool in summer and warm in winter. During the day, it sleeps there in a nest. In the evening, it will leave the burrow. Here it comes. It's an armadillo!

There are several kinds of armadillos in the world. This one is called a nine-banded armadillo. The bands look like stripes around her middle. With her nose and claws, the armadillo roots up leaves and twigs. She is searching for food— beetles, grubs, and ant eggs. Sometimes she also eats berries or juicy roots.

▼ An armadillo's footprints

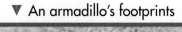

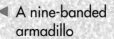
A nine-banded
armadillo

Every now and then the armadillo sits up on her hind legs and listens. She cannot see very well, but she can hear the sounds around her: a leaf rustling, a twig breaking—even a camera clicking.

She also stops to sniff the air. Her keen sense of smell makes up for her poor eyesight. She can follow the trail of a cricket just by sniffing. Now she smells fire ants.

The armadillo starts to dig. Her long claws make her an expert digger. Then she sniffs the hole she has dug, searching for ant eggs. Ants walk along her nose. They try to bite her, but they cannot pierce her tough, leathery covering. This covering is called a carapace, and it protects her body like armor. *Armadillo* is a Spanish word meaning "little armored one." But the armadillo does have some soft spots—the skin on her belly, the skin between her bands, and the tip of her nose, for instance.

The armadillo's long, sticky tongue flicks in and out, in and out, lapping up the food she finds. She has small, stubby teeth, but she doesn't use them for chewing or biting or much of anything.

The armadillo is sniffing, looking for food. ▶

▲ An armadillo has a long
sticky tongue.

Soon she ambles on, searching
for more food. She goes into
dense, scrubby areas, where her
carapace lets her slip through
tangles and prickles. Her bands
allow her to bend and turn with
ease. After a while she wanders
too close to a road. Suddenly
there is a flash of headlights.
What does the armadillo do?
She jumps! That's what
armadillos do when they are
startled. Then they run like
crazy. This armadillo is lucky.
The car does not hit her.

QUICK CHECK

LESSON 5 REVIEW

Think about an animal in your
area that is adapted to its
habitat. Describe three of the
animal's adaptations. Tell how
each adaptation helps the
animal survive.

✔ DOUBLE CHECK

SECTION A REVIEW

1. Draw a picture of an animal that is adapted to
   live in a certain place. The place is very warm in
   the summer and cold in the winter. It is covered
   with tall, green grass, but the animal eats the
   berries from thorny bushes. The bushes are
   2 meters (about 6 feet) high. The berries on the
   bushes grow only near the top. The animal is
   a favorite food of a four-legged predator. The
   predator has sharp teeth and lives on the ground.

2. Tell how your animal is adapted to live in
   its habitat.

Which Group?

You've been invited to a friend's birthday party. You go to the toy store to buy a gift. But when you look at the shelves, you find that nothing is in its usual place. Model trains are mixed together with dolls, games, and puzzles.

Of course, a real toy store has all the toys sorted into different groups by the type of toy. Grouping things can help you find what you're looking for, but it can also do much more.

In this section, you'll learn why grouping living things is important. You'll also learn why animals are put in certain groups. In your Science Log, keep a record of what you find out.

1 WHY CLASSIFY ANIMALS?

Suppose you wanted to put all the games in the toy store in groups. You could divide them into board games, card games, and video games. Later, it would be easy to add new games to each group.

If a game is played on a board, you could group it with the board games. Once the game is in a group, other people would know things about it. Even if they didn't read the box, they would know that the game has a board and a set of rules.

When things are grouped, you have information about them. That's because similar things are grouped together. So once you know something about a group, you also know something about everything in that group.

ACTIVITY

How Do You Group Animals?

Scientists group, or *classify*, animals based on features, or *traits*, of the animals. You can find out more about classifying by doing this activity.

MATERIALS

- 8 buttons
- paper
- pencil
- Science Log data sheet

DO THIS

1 Copy the chart.

CLASSIFYING BUTTONS		
Characteristics Used for Classifying	Number of Groups Formed	Name of Each Group
Color	4	red, white, brown, yellow

2 Classify the buttons based on their traits. You may use shape, color, size, or any other feature you can think of.

3 Fill out the chart as you do the activity. Look at the example in the chart to see how to fill it out. Find as many ways as you can to classify the buttons. Record them in your chart.

THINK AND WRITE

1. How does using groups make it easier to find things?

2. **CLASSIFYING/ORDERING** When you classify objects, you put them into groups. All the objects in each group are alike in some way. Look at the shells in the pictures. What characteristics would you use to classify them?

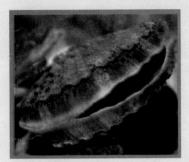
▲ **Scallop**

▲ **Textile cone**

▲ **Imperial thorny oyster**

▲ **Zebra mussels**

▲ **Crown conch**

▲ **Kellet's whelk**

How Scientists Classify

Think about how you grouped the buttons in the last activity. You probably grouped them based on the way they looked. You could see that they were different sizes or colors or had different numbers of holes for attaching them to clothes. Maybe you looked at what the buttons were made from in deciding how to sort them. Whatever trait you chose for sorting, you picked up the next button and sorted it by how it fit into your system.

Scientists classify animals in a similar way. Early scientists placed animals in groups based on what they could observe with their senses. However, the system of classification changed as new facts were discovered. It also changed because better instruments were invented. Scientists were able to observe animals in different ways, even with microscopes. Then they were able to make better classifications based on their observations.

Today scientists have chosen to divide all living things into five large groups called *kingdoms.* All the living things in a kingdom are similar to one another but different from living things in another kingdom. The five kingdoms are the moneran (muh NIR uhn) kingdom, the protist (PROHT ist) kingdom, the fungus kingdom, the plant kingdom, and the animal kingdom. Find out more by looking at the chart on the next page.

Classifying living things helps scientists learn more about them. For example, suppose a scientist in the jungle finds a bird she's never seen before. She studies and observes this bird and classifies it as a kind of parrot. Other scientists will already know many things about this new bird because they know it is a kind of parrot.

▲ How might scientists classify this bird?

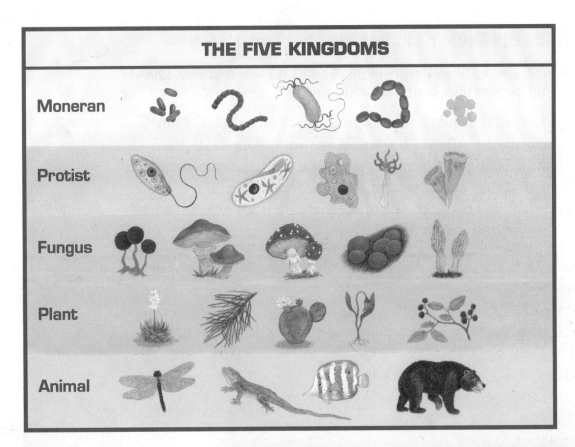

THE FIVE KINGDOMS

Moneran

Protist

Fungus

Plant

Animal

THINK ABOUT IT

Suppose your neighbor has just brought home a cat like the one in the picture. The cat probably looks different from any other cat you've ever seen. Think about what you know about cats. Then tell what you know about your neighbor's cat.

▲ Longhaired Scottish Fold

Naming Animals

Part of classifying living things is naming them. Each type of animal is given its own scientific name.

A scientific name is made of two words often taken from Latin. Scientists all over the world use and understand this one scientific language. Using this scientific language of names, they know that they are all talking about the same animal. Classification also helps scientists share their knowledge and learn from one another.

QUICK CHECK

LESSON 1 REVIEW

Suppose you and a family member have just returned from the grocery store. You bought bread, orange juice, ground beef, frozen vegetables, canned fruits, and milk. Explain how you would group these items.

2 THE ANIMAL KINGDOM

Scientists put all animals in the world into two main groups within the animal kingdom. One of those groups contains all animals that have backbones. The other group contains all the animals that don't have backbones.

Animals with Backbones

Scientists have gathered evidence about animals with backbones. In addition to putting all of the animals with backbones into one group, they have further grouped them as you can see in the diagram.

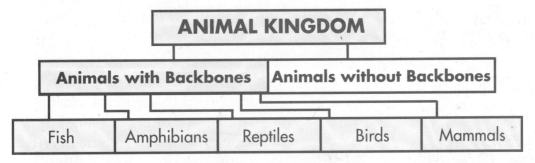

ANIMAL KINGDOM
- Animals with Backbones
- Animals without Backbones

Fish · Amphibians · Reptiles · Birds · Mammals

Why are backbones so important? Look at the pictures on this page, and do the following activity to help you understand.

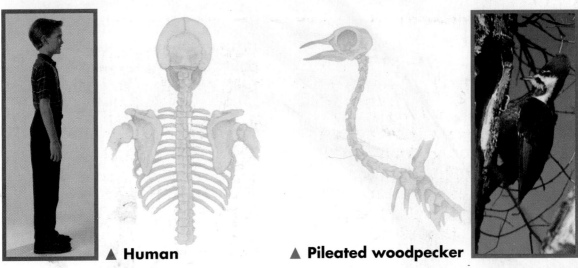

▲ Human   ▲ Pileated woodpecker

Make a Backbone

Bones support, or hold up, your body. They are strong and stiff. They cannot bend. Suppose your backbone were just one piece of bone. How far do you think you could bend? Do this activity to find out how you can bend and turn and move with a backbone.

MATERIALS

- pipe cleaner
- wheel-shaped macaroni
- cotton balls
- Science Log data sheet

DO THIS

1 Bend one end of the pipe cleaner. Thread a piece of macaroni onto the other end. Then push that end of the pipe cleaner through a cotton ball.

2 Put on more macaroni pieces and cotton balls until the pipe cleaner is full. Then bend the straight end of the pipe cleaner.

3 Draw a picture of your backbone. Compare the backbone you made with the picture of the human backbone on page A43.

THINK AND WRITE

1. How is your model like a real backbone?

2. Between the separate bones of your backbone are soft discs. Sometimes these discs get flat or move out of place. When this happens, it hurts to move. Why?

3. **FORMULATING AND USING MODELS** You can't observe your backbone directly because it's inside your body. You made a model of a backbone so you could learn more about a real one. What do the cotton balls and the macaroni stand for in your model?

A Look at Animals with Backbones

You will learn something about a few animals with backbones as you work through this and the following pages.

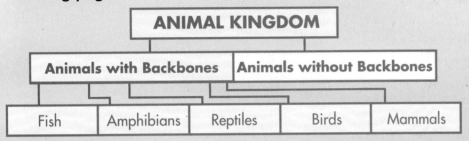

ANIMAL KINGDOM

Animals with Backbones | Animals without Backbones

Fish | Amphibians | Reptiles | Birds | Mammals

Fish

Fish are animals that live in water. Most have scales and fins. Fish use their fins to help them move through the water. They have gills with which to take oxygen from the water.

▲ This tiger shark grows to about 6 meters (20 feet) in length. It uses rows and rows of razor-sharp teeth to capture its prey.

▲ When this porcupine fish is in danger, it gulps water and swells up. Why do you think it does this?

Amphibians

Amphibians (am FIB ee uhnz) are animals that live part of their lives underwater and part of their lives on land. Most amphibians hatch from eggs laid in water. As young animals, amphibians look like fish and take oxygen from the water through gills as fish do. As they get older, they grow legs, and lungs replace their gills. Then they can live on land. But they can also stay underwater for a long time. Amphibians include frogs, toads, salamanders, and newts.

▲ The fire salamander's bright colors are a warning! This amphibian's colors tell predators to stay away.

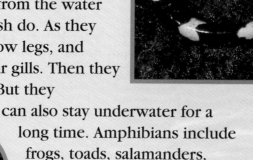

◄ The South African bullfrog breathes with its lungs and through its skin, too. The skin must be moist to take in air.

Reptiles

Reptiles are animals that have scales and that lay eggs with leathery shells. The shells keep their eggs from drying out. So, unlike fish and amphibians, most reptiles can live their whole life on land. Lizards, snakes, turtles, and crocodiles are all reptiles. Some types of reptiles, such as certain snakes and turtles, are adapted to living in water. But even these reptiles lay their eggs on land.

The cobra can squirt poison at its predators. When it's in danger, the cobra spreads out the skin behind its head. This makes it look bigger than it really is. ►

◄ The Galápagos tortoise and other turtles have bony outer shells. They eat both plants and small animals.

Birds

Birds are animals that have feathers, wings, and beaks. They lay eggs with shells. Most birds have wings and feathers that are adapted for flying. Although birds are not the only animals that can fly, they are the only animals that have feathers.

▲ The robin's wing bones are hollow and light. However, other bones help give it support.

The peregrine falcon hunts for and eats other animals. It has a hooked beak for tearing food and long talons for grabbing prey. ▶

Mammals

Mammals are the animals you probably know best. They include cows, horses, deer, bears, and humans. Mammals have fur or hair. The female gives milk from her own body to her young. With most mammals, the female gives birth to only a few babies at a time. She takes care of them for a long time after they're born.

▲ Deer have teeth for cutting and grinding grass. Fur covers their body. The mother deer's body produces milk for the fawn.

◀ Dolphins spend their life in the sea. They may look like fish, but they aren't. They breathe air. After a young dolphin is born, it is pushed to the surface. Then it takes its first breath. Like other mammals, the young dolphin gets milk from its mother.

THINK ABOUT IT

What do the animals you just read about have in common? How are they different from one another?

Animals without Backbones

Scientists have also gathered evidence about animals without backbones. They have been further grouped as shown.

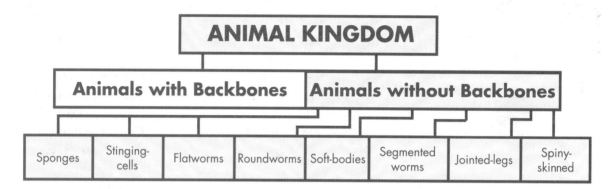

Animals without backbones are found everywhere. They are in the fur of your pets. They are in the dust that settles on the desk. They are crawling in the soil. They are in salt water and in fresh water. Many of them are too small to see. Some of them are very large. Look at the pictures on these pages to see examples of the many kinds of animals without backbones.

◀ Sponge—This animal lives attached to rocks or at the bottom of oceans or in fresh water.

Jellyfish—This animal has stinging cells that help it get food. ▶

▲ Planarian—This is a flatworm that lives in water and feeds on parts of dead animals and plants.

▲ Hookworm—This is a roundworm that lives in soil in the southeastern part of the United States. It can also live inside humans.

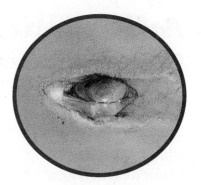

▲ Clam—This soft-bodied animal has a shell to protect it. Other soft-bodied animals, such as an octopus, don't have shells.

▲ Earthworm—This worm's body is divided into rings or segments. It lives in the soil.

▲ Grasshopper—There are many examples of jointed-leg animals. Some of these animals include spiders, horseshoe crabs, millipedes, centipedes, and lobsters.

◀ Starfish—Spiny-skinned animals live in salt water. These animals have tube feet that are used for moving, feeling, and capturing food.

THINK ABOUT IT

Describe two different animals without backbones.

A Big Filing System

Because there are so many kinds of animals, scientists organize them into groups. Then the scientists can study the similarities and differences more easily.

Classification is like a big filing system. Information can be added, taken away, and moved. When does this happen? It happens when new kinds of animals are found. It also happens when scientists make new discoveries about an animal that's already been classified. Then they may decide to classify it in a different group. Can you think of how this might happen?

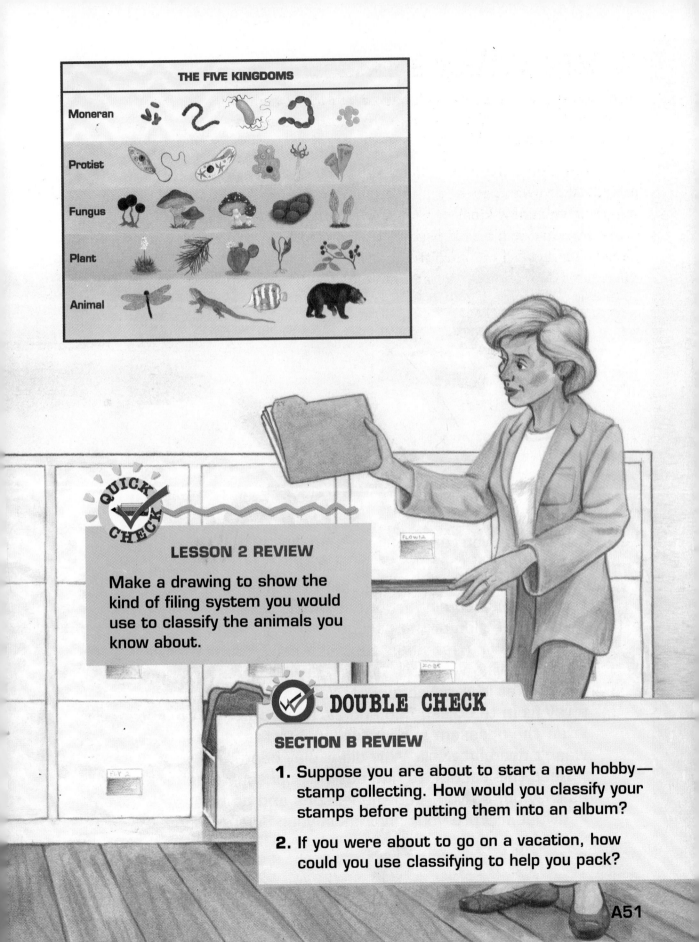

THE FIVE KINGDOMS

Moneran

Protist

Fungus

Plant

Animal

LESSON 2 REVIEW

Make a drawing to show the kind of filing system you would use to classify the animals you know about.

DOUBLE CHECK

SECTION B REVIEW

1. Suppose you are about to start a new hobby—stamp collecting. How would you classify your stamps before putting them into an album?

2. If you were about to go on a vacation, how could you use classifying to help you pack?

SECTION C
How Animals Behave

Suppose you're at a friend's house at the edge of the woods. It is dusk. You and your friend are outside when you hear a rattling noise coming from one of the trash cans by the side of the garage.

What do you see near the trash can? You see an opossum lying very still. In fact, during the entire time you look at it, it never moves. You and your friend walk away from the trash can and sit down quietly. A minute later, the opossum suddenly runs into the woods. It wasn't dead after all. Why did it play dead?

Read this section to find out why opossums behave as they do. As you read the lessons and do the activities, record your findings in your Science Log.

1 ANIMALS DEFEND THEMSELVES

Think about walking on a path through the woods. Sh! Be very quiet. There's a deer by those trees. If it hears you or sees you move, it will run away. Too late! It's heard your footsteps. Off it goes, running away through the trees.

Running Away

You've already read in Section A how some animals hide from predators. The color, pattern, or shape of their bodies acts as camouflage. But some animals do not have camouflage, or their camouflage is not enough protection. Many animals, such as the deer, need other ways to defend themselves.

▲ **A white-tailed deer running through the woods**

You know that body coverings and beaks are adaptations. It might not seem like it, but the way an animal behaves is an adaptation, too!

For many animals, running away is their best defense against danger. One of the fastest runners on Earth is the gazelle. It can run as fast as 100 kilometers per hour (62 miles per hour). That's about the speed that a car travels down a highway. Other animals fly or swim to safety.

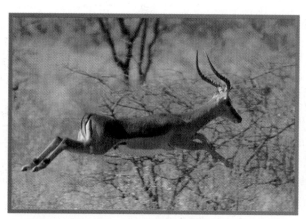

▲ The impala's strong legs help it run from predators.

▲ The bird's wings help it fly to a safe spot.

◀ Animals in the water may swim away from predators.

THINK ABOUT IT

Think about your pet, a friend's pet, or an animal you know something about. Explain how it behaves when it's in danger.

Safety in Numbers

Even fast runners may need other behaviors to stay safe. For some animals, being in a group is safer than being alone.

Giraffes are able to run for hours to escape predators, such as lions. But they also travel in groups as a way of defending themselves. It is more difficult for a lion to pick one giraffe out of an entire group, or herd, of moving animals.

▲ There is safety in numbers for these giraffes.

Zebras stay in a group to protect themselves. The striped pattern of their fur helps them, but only if they are with the rest of their herd. When many zebras are running in a group, they look like a swirl of stripes. This makes it hard for a lion to pick out one animal to catch. Even the very youngest zebras must run with the herd to stay safe. A newborn zebra can join its herd 15 minutes after it's born!

How do the zebra's stripes confuse a predator? ▶

Some animals that can't run fast also stay in groups. Baboons travel in groups of up to 150 animals. Young baboons stay close to their mothers in the center. The much larger and stronger male baboons make a circle around the others. The males will defend the others by screeching to scare away predators. They also have long, pointed teeth with which to attack a predator.

◄ This male baboon protects the others.

The Canadian musk ox is another animal that protects itself by being part of a herd. Herds of musk oxen usually have about 20 to 30 members. The young oxen are prey for wolves. When attacked by wolves, the adult musk oxen form a ring around their young, with their heads facing outward. To reach their prey, the wolves must get past the adult oxen's pointed horns.

▲ The Canadian musk oxen have sharp horns.

The animals you've just read about live in groups all or part of the year. Living in groups helps keep them safe. There are also other reasons these and other animals live in groups. For example, wolves live in packs for safety reasons. But they also help one another survive by hunting for food together and by teaching the pups. The young wolves learn new skills from the adult wolves. This means that the young are more likely to survive. All animals live in groups for more than one reason.

Young wolves learn survival skills from adult wolves. ▼

THINK ABOUT IT

Many years ago, people traveled in covered wagons. At certain times, the people stopped traveling and put the wagons together in a circle. Think about what you just read about the oxen and baboons. Why do you think the travelers put their wagons in a circle?

Stay Away!

Some animals have very interesting behavioral adaptations that help keep them safe. You will see some of them on these pages.

You may recall seeing the photograph of the porcupine fish in Section B. When the porcupine fish is in danger, it puffs up its skin. This makes its spines stick up. So the fish looks larger and more dangerous than it really is.

▲ Both of these photos are of the same porcupine fish. Which one shows the fish trying to scare away a predator?

Have you ever seen a porcupine? Sharp quills cover its body like fur. Each quill is stiff and covered with tiny hooks. If a porcupine cannot run away from danger, it will use its quills. The porcupine backs into the predator. The porcupine's quills easily come off and go into the predator. The tiny hooks on the quills make removing them difficult and painful for the predator.

▲ Quills help protect the porcupine.

◄ You can see the tiny hooks on the quill.

If you've ever smelled a skunk, you know one way it protects itself! Sacs under its tail hold a very strong-smelling liquid. The skunk may stamp its feet or rise up on its front paws as a warning to predators. But if a predator tries to approach, the skunk turns around, raises its tail, and sprays. The sprayed liquid has a terrible smell that keeps the predator away. Not only that, the liquid can also burn the predator's eyes.

▲ Most animals learn not to bother skunks so they won't get sprayed.

▲ Even if a predator comes close enough to sniff the opossum, it still will not move.

You read earlier that an opossum can pretend to be dead. That's the opossum's way of staying safe. Few animals will eat the meat of an animal that is already dead. So predators leave the dead-looking opossum alone and go away.

QUICK CHECK

LESSON 1 REVIEW

❶ Why is it important for newborn zebras to get on their feet very quickly?

❷ Choose two animals and compare the ways they defend themselves.

2 ANIMALS MIGRATE

You may have seen geese flying over your home. Where are they going? Why are they flying away?

The Long Journey

Think about the winter landscape in the north. The ground may be covered with snow for months. Not only is it cold, but the snow covers the grass and other plants. There is little to eat. Birds, such as the Canada goose, have trouble staying warm and finding food.

The Canada geese **migrate,** or move, to find warmer weather and food. Other animals, such as Arctic terns, monarch butterflies, and salmon, also migrate.

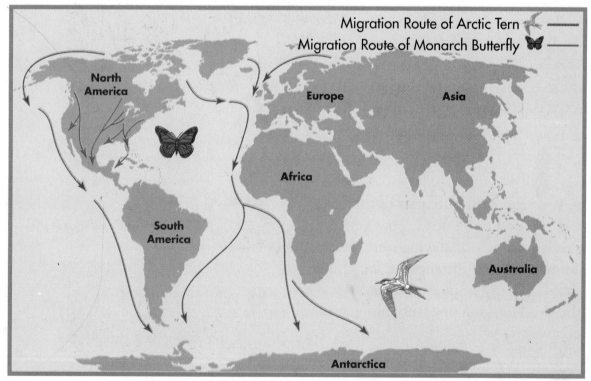

▲ Animals may migrate thousands of kilometers. However, scientists aren't sure exactly how animals know where to go when they migrate. This map shows the migration routes of the Monarch butterfly and the Arctic tern.

A60

In Africa, thousands of wildebeests migrate during the dry season. They travel to the places that have the most rainfall. The areas that get rain have fresh grass—just what the wildebeests need to eat.

◄ Wildebeests migrate to find food and water.

Some animals migrate to find a safe place to lay eggs or raise their young. Salmon hatch from eggs in rivers and streams. Then they swim to the ocean. That's where they spend most of their life. When the salmon are ready to produce young, they return to the place where they were hatched.

THINK ABOUT IT

What are two reasons animals migrate?

▲ Salmon leap over whatever is in their way as they travel upstream back to the place where they were hatched.

ACTIVITY

Canada Geese Get Around

To learn more about Canada geese, scientists have placed bands around the legs of some of these animals. Anyone finding a goose with a band can contact the scientists to tell them where the bird has been seen. In this activity, you'll learn some of the places where Canada geese have been observed.

DO THIS

1 Your teacher will give you an outline map that shows the eastern part of the United States and part of Canada. Fill in the directions north, south, east, and west on your map.

2 Sanctuaries and wildlife areas are places that are kept natural for birds and other wildlife. Find the southern part of James Bay and the Jack Miner Sanctuary on your map. Then find these wildlife areas on your map: Pymatuning, Pee Dee, Carolina Sandhills, and Santee. Use your green pencil to fill in each of these five places on your map.

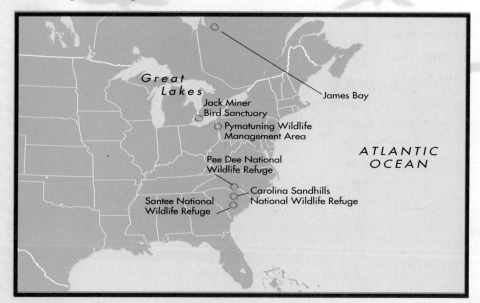

A62

3 The James Bay group of Canada geese flies all the way from the southern part of James Bay to the Carolina Sandhills National Wildlife Refuge. On the way south, part of this group stops at the Jack Miner Bird Sanctuary, and the others stop at Pymatuning. The geese always use these same paths, or flyways, as they travel. Use your blue pencil to draw in their flyways.

THINK AND WRITE

1. Where do the geese go in the north? What is the southernmost point to which they fly?

2. Canada geese spend the spring and summer in the north. In the fall, they fly south. How do you think this helps them survive?

3. **INFERRING** Inferring is using what you have observed to explain something. In this activity, you were asked to record data on a map. Now look at your map. What can you infer about the migration of the Canada geese?

Looking Ahead Perhaps you'd like to find out more about migration. On the following page, you'll have a chance to read about a person who knows a lot about migration. He works at the Jack Miner Bird Sanctuary.

Kirk Miner
Bird Sanctuary Worker

Think of having 20,000 geese and ducks appear in your back yard. That's what happens every year to Kirk Miner. His "yard" is the Jack Miner Sanctuary, in Kingsville, Ontario, Canada.

A bird sanctuary is an area where birds are protected by law from hunters. They can find shelter, food, and water in safety. For the geese, the sanctuary is a place to rest and eat as they travel from their nesting grounds in Canada to spend the winter in the United States. Jack Miner, the founder of the bird sanctuary system, began his sanctuary in 1904. Kirk Miner is the grandson of Jack Miner.

Kirk Miner and his helpers put aluminum tags on thousands of birds each year. "We tag them to find out where the birds migrate to," explains Miner. "We also use the tags to find out how long the birds live." Each tag has a number and the address of the sanctuary. The tag asks people who find the bird to send a postcard telling Miner the number on the tag and where the bird was found.

Students at a nearby school help Miner tag birds. The taggers attract birds into a large net built over the water. They use corn and barley to get the birds inside the net. Once the birds are inside, the taggers quickly slip the tags on the birds' legs and clamp them in place.

Miner and his family live at the Jack Miner Sanctuary. "We feel that we're doing something important," says Miner. "We're giving the birds a place with food, water, and protection that they can return to for many years to come."

QUICK CHECK

LESSON 2 REVIEW

Write a short paragraph that explains why animals migrate.

3 ANIMALS HIBERNATE

Have you ever awakened on a cold morning and just wanted to stay in your nice, warm bed? Staying in bed and going back to sleep is a little bit like what some animals do during winter. Other animals do more than sleep—they hibernate. Read on to find out more.

A Deep Sleep Through Winter

Some animals don't migrate when the weather turns cold. They stay in the same place all year.

Instead of leaving, these animals **hibernate.** They curl up in their nest or some other shelter and go into a state that is deeper than sleep. They may stay there without moving for the whole winter. An animal prepares for hibernation by eating a lot of food. That way, it can survive a long time without eating.

When an animal hibernates, its body gets much colder than usual. It breathes more slowly, and its heart even beats more slowly. Hibernation ends when warm weather arrives and the animal wakes up and begins to look for food.

The dormouse hibernates curled up in its nest. ▶

▲ Most bear cubs are born during the mother bear's winter sleep.

Some animals, such as bears, go into a deep sleep that is like hibernation, but not exactly the same. Their bodies get cold, but their hearts do not slow way down. If there is a sudden warm spell, they may wake up and look for food. Then they might go back to sleep.

While some animals hibernate through the winter, others must find different ways to survive. On the following pages, you'll find out how some animals in Yellowstone National Park live through the winter.

THINK ABOUT IT

Why do you think some animals hibernate rather than migrate?

Surviving Through Winter

Scientists have learned a lot about how animals survive cold weather by observing them during the winter. Read the following article to find out more.

Only the
TOUGH Survive

by **James Halfpenny**
from *Ranger Rick*

LITERATURE Winter is a great time for a scientist like me to spy on wild animals. And my favorite place to check them out is Yellowstone National Park. Snow turns the park into a wonderland. And everything is so peaceful in winter. That's because most visitors stay away when the snow gets deep.

Yellowstone
National Park

◄ The snow is knee deep and the air is way below freezing. How are the animals in Yellowstone surviving?

This big moose is right at home in a winter storm. Deep snow doesn't stop him from walking along. And he's always on the lookout for willow branches to nibble. ►

A67

I'm always amazed at how well some animals survive in weather that's 40° below zero. And I'm not talking about the *hibernators*—the ones that sleep the winter away deep inside their burrows. Lots of other animals, such as the moose, survive in weather so cold you could barely stand it. How do they do it?

A Thick, White Blanket

One way to survive is to use the snow as a blanket. When mice dig tunnels under the snow, the snow keeps their body heat from escaping into the cold outside air. The snow also keeps the bitter-cold wind away from them. So the mice are *much* warmer inside their snow tunnels than they would be outside. The blanket of snow also helps the mice hide from their enemies.

Mice live beneath the snow all winter long. They build their tunnels along the surface of the ground. They use the tunnels to get from one place to another and to find food. It's so dark in the tunnels that the mice can't see anything. They travel blindly, feeling the sides of the tunnels with their whiskers.

▲ This frosty bison shows what happens when steam from the geysers freeze on its coat.

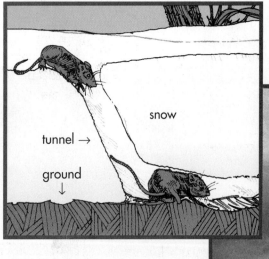

◄ The mouse's tunnel goes down to and along the surface of the ground. When the mouse leaves its tunnel, it has to scramble or it may be caught by a coyote or other predator.

Once in a while, a mouse comes to the surface of the snow. It may need a breath of fresh air. And it may want to check to see whether spring has come. Or, if its tunnel runs into a hard ice wall, the mouse may come up to look for softer snow. Then it will start digging a new tunnel.

If the mouse gets too cold while it's outside, it quickly digs into the snow. In its tiny snow cave, the mouse warms up. Then it can continue its trip.

Mice usually wait till it's dark out before they leave their tunnels. That way their enemies are less likely to catch them. But a dark-colored mouse on white snow is still pretty easy for owls and coyotes to see, even at night. So watch out, mice!

Diving into Tunnels

Even *under* the snow, mice aren't safe from enemies—especially when the snow is shallow and soft. Coyotes hunt for them by listening for tiny squeaks. When a coyote hears a squeak, it springs high into the air. Then it dives nose-first through the soft snow. Sometimes the coyote comes up with a mouse in its mouth. Often it misses, though. And if the snow is deep or the surface is icy, the coyote may go hungry.

◀ For the white-tailed deer, it's tough going. The deer's small feet sink deep into the snow.

Snow Sinkers

Large animals are too big to run around in tunnels under the snow. So they have to do the best they can on the surface. Trouble is, many animals sink into the snow, which really slows them down. And animals that can't move fast often become easy prey. So how do big animals survive when deep snow is everywhere?

Moose can pull their long legs out of chest-deep snow as they walk. And they can stand on their hind legs to nibble high branches. But elk, deer, and bison have to struggle as much as we do when *we* try to walk through deep snow. And the snow makes finding food even harder for these animals. The grass they like to eat may be buried under deep snow. Here's what trying to find food in winter is like for them:

Pretend you're an elk. Now imagine that a box of cereal is all the food you have for one year. In spring, when there's plenty of grass, it's like eating the cereal inside the box. But in winter, you have to start eating the dried stalks of grass. Yuk—that's almost like eating the box the cereal came in. And if spring is late, there's nothing left to eat, and you may die.

So when fresh grass appears in spring—hurray! It's as if you had a new box of cereal to eat.

▲ Fluffy, furry feet help the lynx and the snowshoe hare skim across the top of the snow.

Feet Made for Snow

It's much easier to walk on top of the snow than through it. And having big feet helps keep an animal from sinking in. Take snowshoe hares, for example. Their huge, furry feet help them travel fast on the surface to escape predators.

But—too bad for the hares in Yellowstone—one of their predators *also* has big feet. A lynx can travel on top of the snow just as well as a hare can. Both of them just skim across the surface.

Warm Patches, Hot Steam

The animals that live in some parts of Yellowstone are lucky. No matter how cold it gets, patches of ground in the park stay warm. Why? Long ago, hot melted rocks from deep inside the Earth moved close to the surface. Those hot rocks keep patches of ground warm.

When snow falls on these warm patches, it melts. And in spring, fresh grass gets an early start there. So animals like to gather on the warm patches to rest and eat.

The Earth's hot rocks also heat underground water. This water then shoots into the air as *geysers.* Steam from the geysers sprays everywhere. Bison, deer, elk, and many other animals like to stand in the steam and warm up.

Yellowstone is unlike any other place on Earth. That's why it's such a *great* place to study animals in winter.

▲ Warm patches of ground near Old Faithful and other geysers are great places to find food in winter.

LESSON 3 REVIEW

Why don't animals need to eat during hibernation?

DOUBLE CHECK

SECTION C REVIEW

1. How do the adaptations of hibernating and migrating help animals survive in winter?

2. What are some adaptations of animals in your area that help them survive either in winter or in summer?

Animals Grow and Change

Piglets, calves, and chicks all grow and change as they get older. How do different animals start out? How do they grow and change?

You're different from the way you were last year. And next year you'll change even more as you grow. Look at people and other animals around you. How are they changing? Jot down notes in your Science Log as you read this section and do the investigations.

1 ANIMALS AND THEIR YOUNG

Have you ever visited a hospital nursery for newborn babies? There you see babies lying in their cribs. The babies are all different in certain ways. Some are skinny and some are chubby. Some have hair and some do not. Some have their eyes open and others have theirs closed. Some wiggle around while others lie still.

Born Live

Although human babies all have differences, they also have one thing in common. They are all born live from their mothers' bodies.

Before it is born, the baby-to-be grows inside its mother's body from a tiny speck too small to be seen. Until the baby is developed enough to be born, the mother's body protects the growing new life and gives it food while it grows. Almost all mammals start life this way. The mammal mothers give birth to live young.

You, too, were once as small as this infant. ▶

A mare
and her foal ▶

There are other types of animals besides mammals that give birth to live young. You may recall from Section B that most fish and reptiles lay eggs. However, there are some kinds of fish and reptiles that give birth to live young.

Some fish, such as this lemon shark, give birth to live young. The eggs stay inside the female shark's body until the young are developed. Then she gives birth to the young. ▶

◀ Some reptiles, including boa constrictors, give birth to live young. The eggs stay inside the female's body until they are ready to hatch.

THINK ABOUT IT

What animals do you know of that are born live?

Hatched from Eggs

You know that chickens and other birds hatch from eggs. But did you know that many other animals also hatch from eggs?

Most animals without backbones and most with backbones hatch from eggs. Hatched animals with backbones include all birds, most fish, most amphibians, and most reptiles. One kind of mammal, the platypus, also hatches from eggs.

▲ These chicks were hatched from eggs.

▲ This green snake is hatching from an egg.

▲ Many insects, such as the grasshopper, lay eggs.

The platypus is an unusual-looking mammal. It is also unusual because it lays eggs. ▼

THINK ABOUT IT

What are some animals you can think of that hatch from eggs?

A75

ACTIVITY

Inside an Egg

Have you ever wanted to find out more about what's inside an egg? Here's your chance!

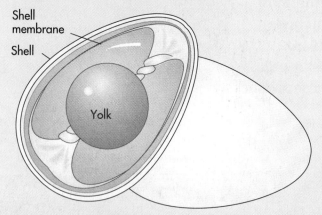

Shell membrane
Shell
Yolk

DO THIS

1 CAUTION: Do not touch the egg with your fingers. Wash your hands after you complete this activity. Your teacher will break open an egg and put it in the bowl.

2 Use the hand lens to look at the parts of the egg. Identify the egg white and the yolk. Look carefully for the small white spot on the yolk. A young chick would grow from this spot.

3 Find the twisted strands in the egg white. What do you think they might do?

4 Use the hand lens to look at the shell and the thin lining of the shell. How do you think the tiny holes in the eggshell help the egg? What might the lining do?

THINK AND WRITE

Draw a picture of your egg. Label the egg yolk, white spot, and egg white. Include the eggshell in your drawing. How does the eggshell protect the egg?

Eggs, Eggs, and More Eggs

In the last activity, you studied the egg of a chicken. The egg was surrounded by a hard shell. Other bird eggs are also covered by a hard shell. What is the purpose of the shell?

The shell gives the young animal a watery home inside the egg while it grows. The shell protects the egg from drying out in the air. It also helps protect the young from being eaten.

Some birds protect their eggs by staying with them in the nest. Many of these birds stay to feed and care for the young birds after they hatch.

Unlike a bird egg, a fish egg has no shell. Fish eggs don't need protection from drying out, because they are laid in water. But they are in danger of being eaten by fish and other predators living in the water.

Emperor penguins have interesting nesting habits. The male penguin keeps the egg warm until it hatches. He rolls the egg onto his feet. Then he covers up the egg with the lower part of his belly. The male penguins huddle together in a group to keep themselves and the eggs warm. After the egg hatches, both parents look after the young chick. ▶

◄ The female perch protects her eggs by holding them in her mouth. When the young hatch, they stay nearby and swim back into her mouth to escape danger.

To protect their eggs from predators, some types of fish cover the eggs with gravel. Others, such as some types of perch and sea catfish, lay their eggs and then suck the eggs into their mouths. But they don't swallow the eggs. Instead, they hold the eggs in their mouth to keep them from being eaten before they can hatch. Once the eggs hatch, the adult fish lets the young out of its mouth.

Most fish lay many eggs. For example, a cod may lay up to nine million eggs in a single year! Most of the eggs will be eaten by predators. But because there are so many eggs, at least a few of them survive.

▲ Female cod release eggs similar to the orange-colored eggs in this photograph several times a year.

Reptiles lay eggs with shells. The shells of these eggs are not hard like those of bird eggs. Reptile eggs have tough, leathery shells. Like bird eggshells, the leathery shells keep the young from drying out. But unlike bird eggshells, these shells don't crack easily or break. Most reptiles lay their eggs in a warm spot and then leave them alone. Some reptiles, like the loggerhead turtle, bury their eggs in sand on a beach.

Not even all bird eggs are the same. The size of the egg depends on the type of bird. The huge ostrich egg is larger than a grapefruit. But some hummingbird eggs are smaller than a blueberry.

▲ The female loggerhead turtle swims to the shore at night. She crawls up onto the beach to lay her eggs.

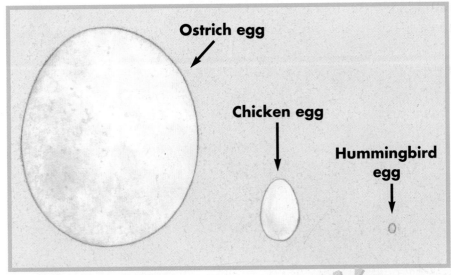

Ostrich egg

Chicken egg

Hummingbird egg

▲ As you can see, eggs vary in size.

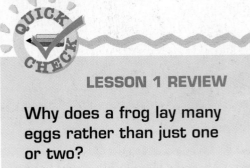

QUICK CHECK

LESSON 1 REVIEW

Why does a frog lay many eggs rather than just one or two?

2 GROWTH AND CHANGE

When you were born, you probably weighed no more than 4 kilograms (about 9 pounds). You probably had little or no hair and you didn't know how to speak. You've changed a lot since then.

From Kitten to Cat

All animals grow and change. Here's how a kitten grows from a newborn to an adult cat.

When a kitten is born, its mother licks it clean. Its eyes and ears are sealed shut. The kitten cannot see or hear. It can't do anything by itself except nurse, or suck milk from its mother.

▲ The one-day-old kitten is blind and helpless.

▲ Each kitten nurses at the same place each time. While the kittens nurse, the mother cat observes her kittens and often cleans them.

Cats usually give birth to a litter, or group, of about three to five kittens. By the second day, a newborn kitten begins to show fluffy fur. Even though it's still blind, it knows who its mother is. The kitten knows her smell and can feel her warmth and her purring. The kitten spends most of its time nursing and sleeping.

The kitten is now ready to see the world around it. But it's still too helpless to move away from its mother. The kitten needs its mother to feed and clean it.

▲ The newborn kitten depends upon its mother for all of its needs.

When a kitten is a little more than 2 weeks old, it begins to crawl. It's just beginning to learn about the world away from its mother.

By the time the kitten is 3 weeks old, it can walk around and explore. But the mother cat doesn't let it go too far. Before the kitten can get lost, the mother picks it up by the skin on its neck and brings it back to safety.

At 4 weeks, the kitten begins to explore and play. Kittens pile on top of one another and roll around. They play hide-and-seek with a paper bag. And they love to play with toys. But watch out! They think everything you own is a toy, including your homework!

▲ The 15-day-old kitten is beginning to crawl, but it is very wobbly.

The kitten is beginning to care for itself. ▶

Kittens spend time playing together. ▼

The kitten also learns to take care of its other needs. By this time, the kitten has a full set of first teeth. It can start to eat solid food. The kitten also learns to wash its fur, just as its mother has done for it since it was born.

The kitten is beginning to explore new places. ▶

By the time it is 8 weeks old, a kitten may stop nursing. Instead, it eats solid food and drinks water from a dish. And it is very busy playing. The games kittens play help them practice skills such as sneaking up on prey and catching it. These are skills they may need as adult cats.

While kittens play, they are also learning hunting skills they may use when they're adults. ▶

When a kitten is 6 months old, it looks like a small adult cat. It can take care of itself without its mother. Most cats are fully grown by the time they're 1 year old.

This kitten is 6 months old. ▼

This cat is 1 year old. It is fully grown. Compare this picture to the other kitten pictures. See how the kitten has grown and developed! ▼

THINK ABOUT IT

How does a mother cat help her young stay healthy?

Match the Animals

When kittens are born, they don't look exactly like their mother. But you can still tell that a kitten is a young cat. A kitten is born to an adult cat, not to an adult dog. All young animals come from the same kind of adult animal that they will grow into. Try to match these young animals with the adults they will become.

Look at each picture. Find two pictures that show the same type of animal—one an adult and one its young. In your Science Log, write down the name of each animal. Next to each name, write the numbers of the two pictures of that animal.

THINK ABOUT IT

1. What are some ways in which these young animals look different from their parents?

2. What are some ways that these young animals are like their parents?

3. **CLASSIFYING/ORDERING**
When you classify objects, you put them into groups according to ways they are alike. What information did you use to group the animals in the pictures as adults and young of the same kind?

Insects Grow and Change

You probably noticed in the Match the Animals pictures on pages A84–A85 that the young frog did not look like the adult. You would find it very difficult to match a picture of the young of some animals to a picture of their parents. Not all young animals look like adult animals of the same kind. One such animal is an insect called a *mealworm*. A mealworm hatches from an egg. To find out more about how a mealworm changes as it grows, try this activity.

MATERIALS

- oatmeal
- plastic bowl with lid
- apple or potato slices
- 5 mealworms
- hand lens
- Science Log data sheet

DO THIS ⚙CAUTION

❶ Put about 2 cm of oatmeal in the bottom of the bowl. Place an apple or potato slice in the bowl, too.

❷ Using the hand lens, look at the mealworms.

❸ CAUTION: Wash your hands after touching the mealworms. Put the mealworms in the bowl. Then put the lid on the bowl.

❹ Copy the chart below three times. Label one chart *Week 1*, one *Week 2*, and one *Week 3*.

MEALWORM GROWTH		
Week 1		
Day	Amount of Food Eaten	Observations About the Mealworms
1		
2		
3		
4		
5		

❺ Observe the mealworms every school day for 3 weeks. Record your observations in the charts.

❻ Add more oatmeal and a fresh apple or potato slice every 2 days.

THINK AND WRITE

1. Draw pictures or write a paragraph describing how the mealworms changed over the 3 weeks.

2. **INFERRING** Inferring is using what you have observed to explain what has happened. You have recorded your observations about mealworms in your charts. Look at your charts and explain what you observed. From your observations and data, what can you infer about the growth of mealworms?

From Egg to Butterfly

You've just seen how a mealworm grows and changes. Now follow the pictures to see how another kind of insect changes.

◄ **1** Butterflies lay eggs on a leaf.

◄ **2** A caterpillar hatches from the egg. It begins to eat and grow. This caterpillar will someday become a monarch butterfly!

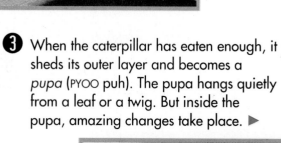

3 When the caterpillar has eaten enough, it sheds its outer layer and becomes a *pupa* (PYOO puh). The pupa hangs quietly from a leaf or a twig. But inside the pupa, amazing changes take place. ►

◄ **4** After several weeks, the skin of the pupa splits and the butterfly starts to come out.

5 At first, the butterfly's wings are damp. Soon the wings will dry and harden. ▼

6 The monarch butterfly is now fully grown! ▼

LESSON 2 REVIEW

How do animals and insects change as they grow?

DOUBLE CHECK

SECTION D REVIEW

1. How were you similar to a newborn kitten when you were born? How are the ways that you change as you grow like the ways a kitten changes?

2. How is the way you began life different from the way a chick begins life? How are the ways you change different from the ways a chick changes?

3. How are the eggs of birds, fish, and reptiles the same? How are they different?

I REFLECT

It's time to think about the ideas you have discovered during your investigations. Think, too, about your many accomplishments.

SUMMARIZE

Answer the following in your Science Log.

1. What **I Wonder** questions have you answered in your investigations? What new questions have you asked?

2. What have you discovered about animals? How have your ideas changed?

3. Did any of your discoveries surprise you? Explain.

ANIMALS I SAW IN MY NEIGHBORHOOD		
Animal	Group	Body Covering
dog	mammal	skin with fur
frog	amphibian	skin
pigeon	bird	skin with feathers

CONNECT IDEAS

1. Some animals, such as cats, have eyes in the front of their heads. How does this adaptation help the animals hunt?

2. Rabbits have large ears. How does this adaptation help rabbits survive?

3. How do animals in your part of the country spend the winter?

4. Think about the many changes in a kitten as it grows. How is the way a kitten grows like the way you are growing and changing?

SCIENCE PORTFOLIO

❶ Complete your Science Experiences Record.

❷ Choose one or two samples of your best work from each section to include in your Science Portfolio.

❸ On A Guide to My Science Portfolio, tell why you chose each sample.

I SHARE

Scientists share their discoveries and ideas and learn from one another. How can you share what you've learned?

Decide

► what you want to say.

► what the best way is to get your message across.

Share

► what you did and why.

► what worked and what didn't work.

► what conclusions you have drawn.

► what else you'd like to find out.

Find Out

► what classmates liked about what you shared—and why.

► what questions your classmates have.

I ACT

Science is more than discoveries—it is also what you do with those discoveries. How might you use what you have learned about all types of animals?

▶ Litter can harm animals. Start a campaign in your class against littering.

▶ Make a poster showing how some of the animals found in your area are classified.

▶ Invite a veterinarian to speak about animals to your class.

▶ Choose one animal. Then write sentences and draw pictures for a book about how this animal grows and changes. Read your book to a younger child.

THE LANGUAGE OF SCIENCE

The language of science helps people communicate clearly when they talk about nature. Here are some vocabulary words you can use when you talk about animals with friends, family, and others.

▲ Elephants have several adaptations that help them survive.

camouflage—coloring, shape, or pattern that helps an animal blend into its surroundings. **(A23)**

▲ This ringed plover is camouflaged when it crouches among the rocks.

adaptation—any trait that helps an animal survive in its surroundings. Adaptations include body coverings, body parts such as beaks and teeth, camouflage, and behavior. **(A20)**

▲ A cat's behavior can help keep it safe from predators.

classify—to group things by their characteristics. Scientists have classified all living things into kingdoms. **(A38)**

habitat—the place where an animal lives because it finds the kind of food and shelter it needs. **(A23)**

hibernate—an animal's long, deep "sleep" that allows it to survive the winter. During hibernation the animal's breathing and heartbeat slow down. Some mice, bats, ground squirrels, and a few other animals hibernate. **(A65)**

▲ Animals such as this ground squirrel hibernate during the winter.

migrate—what animals do when they travel from one area to another and back each year or season. Many birds migrate each winter. Some insects, such as monarch butterflies, also migrate to find warmer weather or food. **(A60)**

predator—an animal that hunts and eats other animals. **(A21)**

prey—an animal that is eaten by another animal. **(A21)**

trait—a characteristic or feature of a living thing. Some traits of a falcon are a strong beak, brown feathers, excellent eyesight, and sharp talons. **(A38)**

A falcon is well equipped for hunting. ▼

▲ Some animals migrate to avoid hot weather. The bogong moths of Australia migrate to cool mountain caves during the hot, dry months.

REFERENCE HANDBOOK

Safety in the Classroom

Doing activities in science can be fun, but you need to be sure you do them safely. It is up to you, your teacher, and your classmates to make your classroom a safe place for science activities.

Think about what causes most accidents in everyday life—being careless, not paying attention, and showing off. The same kinds of behavior cause accidents in the science classroom.

Here are some ways to make your classroom a safe place.

THINK AHEAD.

Study the steps of the activity so you know what to expect. If you have any questions about the steps, ask your teacher to explain. Be sure you understand any safety symbols that are shown in the activity.

WATCH YOUR EYES.

Wear safety goggles anytime you are directed to do so. If you should ever get any substance in your eyes, tell your teacher right away.

BE NEAT.

Keep your work area clean. If you have long hair, pull it back so it doesn't get in the way. If you have long sleeves, roll them or push them up to keep them away from your experiment.

OOPS!

If you should have an accident that causes a spill or breaks something, or if you get cut, tell your teacher right away.

YUCK!

Never eat or drink anything during a science activity unless you are told to do so by your teacher.

KEEP IT CLEAN.

Always clean up when you have finished your activity. Put everything away and wipe your work area. Last of all, wash your hands.

DON'T GET SHOCKED.

Sometimes you need to use electric appliances, such as lamps, in an activity. You always need to be careful around electricity. Be sure that electric cords are in a safe place where you can't trip over them. Don't ever pull a plug out of an outlet by pulling on the cord.

Safety Symbols

In some activities, you will see a symbol that stands for what you need to do to stay safe. Do what the symbol stands for.

 This is a general symbol that tells you to be careful. Reading the steps of the activity will tell you exactly what you need to do to be safe.

 You will need to protect your eyes if you see this symbol. Put on safety goggles and leave them on for the entire activity.

 This symbol tells you that you will be using something sharp in the activity. Be careful not to cut or poke yourself or others.

 This symbol tells you something hot will be used in the activity. Be careful not to get burned or to cause someone else to get burned.

 This symbol tells you to put on an apron to protect your clothing.

 Don't touch! This symbol tells you that you will need to touch something that is hot. Use a thermal mitt to protect your hand.

 This symbol tells you that you will be using electric equipment. Use proper safety procedures.

Using a Hand Lens

A hand lens magnifies objects, or makes them look larger than they are.

▲ This object is not in focus.

Sometimes objects are too small for you to see easily without some help. You might want to see details that you cannot see with your eyes alone. When this happens, you can use a hand lens.

To use a hand lens, first place the object you want to look at on a flat surface, such as a table. Next, hold the hand lens over the object. At first, the object may appear blurry, like the object in **A**. Move the hand lens toward or away from the object until the object comes into sharp focus, as shown in **B**.

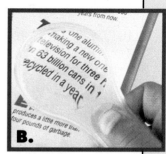

▲ This object is focused clearly.

Making a Water-Drop Lens

There may be times when you want to use a hand lens but there isn't one around. If that happens, you can make a water-drop lens to help you in the same way a hand lens does. A water-drop lens is best used to make flat objects, such as pieces of paper and leaves, seem larger.

MATERIALS
• sheet of acetate
• 2 rectangular rubber erasers
• water
• dropper

DO THIS

❶ Place the object to be magnified on a table between two identical erasers.

❷ Place a sheet of acetate on top of the erasers so that the sheet of acetate is about 1 cm above the object.

❸ Use the dropper to place one drop of water on the surface of the sheet over the object. Don't make the drop too large or it will make things look bent.

A water-drop lens can magnify objects. ▶

Caring For and Using a Microscope

A microscope, like a hand lens, magnifies objects. However, a microscope can increase the detail you see by increasing the number of times an object is magnified.

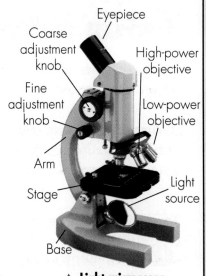

▲ **Light microscope**

CARING FOR A MICROSCOPE

- Always use two hands when you carry a microscope.
- Never touch any of the lenses of the microscope with your fingers.

USING A MICROSCOPE

1 Raise the eyepiece as far as you can using the coarse-adjustment knob. Place the slide you wish to view on the stage.

2 Always start by using the lowest power. The lowest-power lens is usually the shortest. Start with the lens in the lowest position it can go without touching the slide.

3 Look through the eyepiece and begin adjusting the eyepiece upward with the coarse-adjustment knob. When the slide is close to being in focus, use the fine-adjustment knob.

4 When you want to use the higher-power lens, first focus the slide under low power. Then, watching carefully to make sure that the lens will not hit the slide, turn the higher-power lens into place. Use only the fine-adjustment knob when looking through the higher-power lens.

Some of you may use a Brock microscope. This is a sturdy microscope that has only one lens.

1 Place the object to be viewed on the stage. Move the long tube, containing the lens, close to the stage.

2 Put your eye on the eyepiece, and begin raising the tube until the object comes into focus.

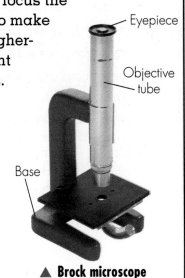

▲ **Brock microscope**

Using a Dropper

Use a dropper when you need to add small amounts of a liquid to another material.

A dropper has two main parts. One is a large empty part called a *bulb*. You hold the bulb and squeeze it to use the dropper. The other part of a dropper is long and narrow and is called a *tube*.

DO THIS

1 Use a clean dropper for each liquid you measure.

2 With the dropper out of the liquid, squeeze the bulb and keep it squeezed. Then dip the end of the tube into the liquid.

3 Release the pressure on the bulb. As you do so, you will see the liquid enter the tube.

▲ **Using a dropper correctly**

4 Take the dropper from the liquid, and move it to the place you want to put the liquid. If you are putting the liquid into another liquid, do not let the dropper touch the surface of the second liquid.

5 Gently squeeze the bulb until one drop comes out of the tube. Repeat slowly until you have measured out the right number of drops.

▲ **Using a dropper incorrectly**

Measuring Liquids

Use a beaker, a measuring cup, or a graduated cylinder to measure liquids accurately.

Containers for measuring liquids are made of clear or translucent materials so that you can see the liquid inside them. On the outside of each of these measuring tools, you will see lines and numbers that make up a scale. On most of the containers used by scientists, the scale is in milliliters (mL).

DO THIS

1 Pour the liquid you want to measure into one of the measuring containers. Make sure your measuring container is on a flat, stable surface, with the measuring scale facing you.

2 Look at the liquid through the container. Move so that your eyes are even with the surface of the liquid in the container.

3 To read the volume of the liquid, find the scale line that is even with the top of the liquid. In narrow containers, the surface of the liquid may look curved. Take your reading at the lowest point of the curve.

▲ There are 32 mL of liquid in this graduated cylinder.

4 Sometimes the surface of the liquid may not be exactly even with a line. In that case, you will need to estimate the volume of the liquid. Decide which line the liquid is closer to, and use that number.

▲ There are 27 mL of liquid in this beaker.

Using a Thermometer

Determine temperature readings of the air and most liquids by using a thermometer with a standard scale.

Most thermometers are thin tubes of glass that are filled with a red or silver liquid. As the temperature goes up, the liquid in the tube rises. As the temperature goes down, the liquid sinks. The tube is marked with lines and numbers that provide a temperature scale in degrees. Scientists use the Celsius scale to measure temperature. A temperature reading of 27 degrees Celsius is written 27°C.

DO THIS

❶ Place the thermometer in the liquid whose temperature you want to record, but don't rest the bulb of the thermometer on the bottom or side of the container. If you are measuring the temperature of the air, make sure that the thermometer is not in direct sunlight or in line with a direct light source.

❷ Move so that your eyes are even with the liquid in the thermometer.

❸ If you are measuring a material that is not being heated or cooled, wait about two minutes for the reading to become stable. Find the scale line that meets the top of the liquid in the thermometer, and read the temperature.

❹ If the material you are measuring is being heated or cooled, you will not be able to wait before taking your measurements. Measure as quickly as you can.

The temperature of this liquid is 27°C. ▶

Making a Thermometer

If you don't have a thermometer, you can make a simple one easily. The simple thermometer won't give you an exact temperature reading, but you can use it to tell if the temperature is going up or going down.

MATERIALS

- small, narrow-mouthed jar
- colored water
- clear plastic straw
- ruler
- clay
- dropper
- pen, pencil, or marker
- bowl of ice
- bowl of warm water

DO THIS

1. Add colored water to the jar until it is nearly full.

2. Place the straw in the jar. Finish filling the jar with water, but leave about 1 cm of space at the top.

3. Lift the straw until 10 cm of it stick up out of the jar. Use the clay to seal the mouth of the jar.

4. Use the dropper to add colored water to the straw until the straw is at least half full.

5. On the straw, mark the level of the water. "S" stands for *start*.

6. To get an idea of how your thermometer works, place the jar in a bowl of ice. Wait several minutes, and then mark the new water level on the straw. This new water level should be marked C for *cold*.

7. Take the jar out of the bowl of ice, and let it return to room temperature. Next, place the jar in a bowl of warm water. Wait several minutes, and then mark the new water level on the straw. This level can be labeled W for *warm*.

▶ You can use a thermometer like this to decide if the temperature of a liquid or the air is going up or down.

Using a Balance

Use a balance to measure an object's mass. Mass is the amount of matter an object has.

Most balances look like the one shown. They have two pans. In one pan, you place the object you want to measure. In the other pan, you place standard masses. Standard masses are objects that have a known mass. Grams are the units used to measure mass for most scientific activities.

DO THIS

1 First, make certain the empty pans are balanced. They are in balance if the pointer is at the middle mark on the base. If the pointer is not at this mark, move the slider to the right or left. Your teacher will help if you cannot balance the pans.

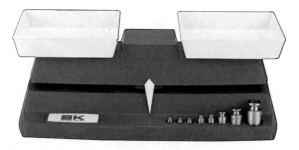

◀ **These pans are balanced and ready to be used to find the mass of an object.**

2 Place the object you wish to measure in one pan. The pointer will move toward the pan without the object in it.

3 Add the standard masses to the other pan. As you add masses, you should see the pointer begin to move. When the pointer is at the middle mark again, the pans are balanced.

4 Add the numbers on the masses you used. The total is the mass of the object you measured.

These pans are unbalanced. ▶

Making a Balance

If you do not have a balance, you can make one. A balance requires only a few simple materials. You can use nonstandard masses such as paper clips or nickels. This type of balance is best for measuring small masses.

DO THIS

MATERIALS
- 1 sturdy plastic or wooden ruler
- string
- transparent tape
- 2 paper cups
- 2 large paper clips

1 If the ruler has holes in it, tie the string through the center hole. If it does not have holes, tie the string around the middle of the ruler.

2 Tape the other end of the string to a table. Allow the ruler to hang down from the side of the table. Adjust the ruler so that it is level.

3 Unbend the end of each paper clip slightly. Push these ends through the paper cups as shown. Attach each cup to the ruler by using the paper clips.

4 Adjust the cups until the ruler is level again.

▶ **This balance is ready for use.**

Using a Spring Scale

A spring scale is a tool you use to measure the force of gravity on objects. You find the weight of the objects and use newtons as the unit of measurement for the force of gravity. You also use the spring scale and newtons to measure other forces.

A spring scale has two main parts. One part is a spring with a hook on the end. The hook is used to connect an object to the spring scale. The other part is a scale with numbers that tell you how many newtons of force are acting on the object.

DO THIS

With an Object at Rest

With the object resting on the table, hook the spring scale to it. Do not stretch the spring at this point.

Lift the scale and object with a smooth motion. Do not jerk them upward.

Wait until any motion in the spring comes to a stop. Then read the number of newtons from the scale.

With an Object in Motion

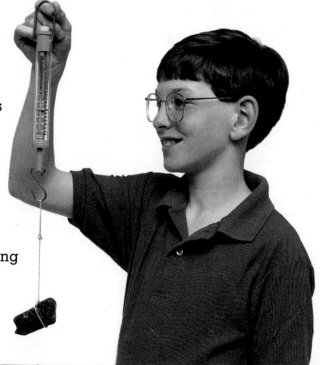

With the object resting on the table, hook the spring scale to it. Do not stretch the spring.

Pull the object smoothly across the table. Do not jerk the object. If you pull with a jerky motion, the spring scale will wiggle too much for you to get a good reading.

As you are pulling, read the number of newtons you are using to pull the object.

Making a Spring Scale

If you do not have a spring scale, you can make one by following the directions below.

DO THIS

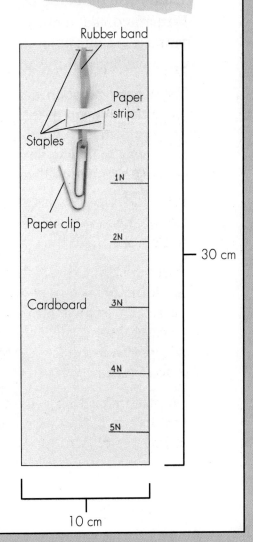
1 Staple one end of the rubber band (the part with the sharp curve) to the middle of one end of the cardboard so that the rubber band hangs down the length of the cardboard. Color the loose end of the rubber band with a marker to make it easy to see.

2 Bend the paper clip so that it is slightly open and forms a hook. Hang the paper clip by its unopened end from the rubber band.

3 Put the narrow paper strip across the rubber band, and staple the strip to the cardboard. The rubber band and hook must be able to move easily.

4 While holding the cardboard upright, hang one 100-g mass from the hook. Allow the mass to come to rest, and mark the position of the bottom of the rubber band on the cardboard. Label this position on the cardboard 1 N. Add another 100-g mass for a total of 200 g.

5 Continue to add masses and mark the cardboard. Each 100-g mass adds a force of about 1 N.

Rubber band

Paper strip

Staples

Paper clip

Cardboard

1N
2N
3N
4N
5N

30 cm

10 cm

Working Like a Scientist
What Do Rabbits Like to Eat?

Have you ever wanted to know about something but you didn't know how to find out about it? Working like a scientist can help. Read the story below to find out how Alita, Juan, and Jasmine learned to work like scientists.

Alita, Juan, and Jasmine were friends. Each of them owned a rabbit. "I'd like to give my rabbit a treat," Alita told Juan and Jasmine. "I want the treat to be something that my rabbit likes. It should also be good for the rabbit."

"What do you think the best treat would be?" Juan asked.

"That's a good question," Jasmine said. "How can we find out the answer?"

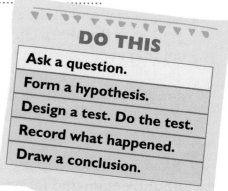

DO THIS

Ask a question.
Form a hypothesis.
Design a test. Do the test.
Record what happened.
Draw a conclusion.

Asking a good question is the first step in working like a scientist. A good question helps you find out what the problem is. A good question starts you on the way to finding an answer. Often a good question will have many answers.

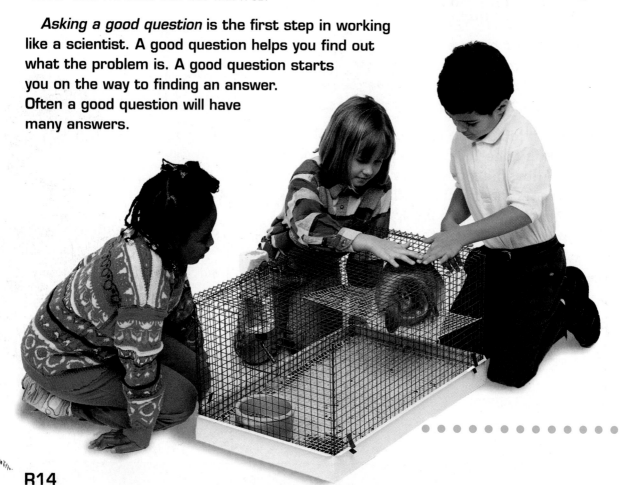

After you ask a good question, you need to choose one possible answer and then find out if your answer is right. This possible answer to your question is called a *hypothesis*. You *form a hypothesis* when you choose an answer to a question. Sometimes you must do research before you can choose an answer. Find out how Alita, Juan, and Jasmine formed their hypothesis.

The next day, Alita, Juan, and Jasmine met at Alita's house. Juan and Jasmine had brought their rabbits in their carrying cages.

"We need to find out what the best treat for a rabbit would be," Juan said.

Alita said, "My grandpa told me that rabbits like all kinds of vegetables. Maybe vegetables would be the best treat."

"I gave my rabbit some celery once and she didn't eat it at all. I wonder if my rabbit is different," Juan replied.

Jasmine said, "Why don't we say that we think rabbits like carrots, celery, and broccoli? Then we could test our rabbits to see if we're right."

"Yes," Alita said. "We can offer each rabbit carrots, celery, and broccoli and see what each one likes best."

"That sounds like a good idea," Juan said.

When Jasmine said to *do a test*, she was talking about doing an experiment. An experiment must be carefully designed and planned. You must decide how to do your test and how to record the results.

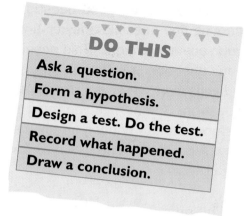

DO THIS

Ask a question.
Form a hypothesis.
Design a test. Do the test.
Record what happened.
Draw a conclusion.

Alita said, "We can put the three kinds of vegetables in each cage. We can watch our rabbits and see which vegetables they eat."

Jasmine said, "But we should do the test when we know our rabbits aren't very hungry. If they were, they might eat anything. I know that when I'm very hungry, I eat anything."

"That's true," Juan said. "And we shouldn't put one vegetable closer to the rabbit than the other vegetables. The rabbit might eat the first vegetable it saw. It might not eat the vegetable it liked best."

Alita said, "That sounds good. Let me write that down."

Jasmine said, "I've been thinking about our test. How are we going to know what the answer is? We should be able to say why we're giving our rabbits a certain kind of treat."

Juan said, "That's a good question. We have to find a way to record what our rabbits do."

Alita smiled. She showed Juan and Jasmine a chart.

"I made up this chart. It has a place for each rabbit and each kind of vegetable. We can see which vegetable each rabbit eats first."

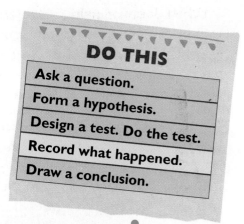

DO THIS

| Ask a question. |
| Form a hypothesis. |
| Design a test. Do the test. |
| Record what happened. |
| Draw a conclusion. |

A Rabbit's Favorite Treat

	Broccoli			Carrots			Celery		
	1st	2nd	3rd	1st	2nd	3rd	1st	2nd	3rd
Jasmine's Rabbit									
Juan's Rabbit									
Alita's Rabbit									

What Alita showed Juan and Jasmine was a way to record what they saw the rabbits do. This is called *recording data*. It is an important part of science because it helps you explain why you think one answer may be right and another may be wrong.

Alita, Juan, and Jasmine put broccoli, carrots, and celery into the three rabbit cages. Alita's rabbit smelled the broccoli and then hopped to the carrots.

The rabbit ate some of the carrots, but it did not eat the celery. Jasmine's rabbit ate the carrots and a little bit of the celery. Juan's rabbit ate only the carrots.

Alita filled in the chart, and the three friends looked at it. Jasmine said, "It looks as if all three rabbits like carrots. My rabbit likes celery. None of the rabbits like broccoli."

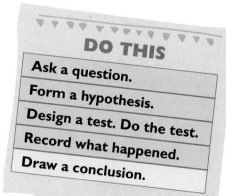

DO THIS

Ask a question.
Form a hypothesis.
Design a test. Do the test.
Record what happened.
Draw a conclusion.

A Rabbit's Favorite Treat	Broccoli			Carrots			Celery		
	1st	2nd	3rd	1st	2nd	3rd	1st	2nd	3rd
Jasmine's Rabbit				X				X	
Juan's Rabbit				X					
Alita's Rabbit				X					

What Jasmine did is *draw a conclusion.* She looked at the results of the test and was able to say what she thought the test showed. Just doing a test is not enough. You must be able to say what the test showed you.

"We haven't tried all vegetables," Juan said.

"No," Alita said. "And we didn't measure how much of the carrots and celery Jasmine's rabbit ate."

"We can do more tests," Jasmine said.

"All right," Alita said. "That would be fun!"

Juan said, "But for now, we know that our rabbits like carrots. So we can give them carrots for treats."

INDEX

Note: Page numbers in italics indicate illustrations.

ACKNOWLEDGMENTS

For permission to reprint copyrighted material, grateful acknowledgment is made to the following sources:

Mel Boring: From "The Bridge That Couldn't Be Built" in *Cricket* Magazine, June 1991. Text © by Mel Boring.

Carolrhoda Books, Inc., Minneapolis, MN: Cover illustration from *How the Guinea Fowl Got Her Spots* by Barbara Knutson. Copyright © 1990 by Barbara Knutson.

Children's Better Health Institute, Indianapolis, IN: From "Magic Jumpson" (originally titled "The Froggie") in *Jack and Jill* Magazine, March 1991. Text copyright © 1988 by Children's Better Health Institute, Benjamin Franklin Literary & Medical Society, Inc.

Coward, McCann & Geoghegan: Abridged from "Amelia Earhart" by Peggy Mann in *Amelia Earhart, First Lady of Flight.* Text copyright © 1970 by Peggy Mann.

Current Health 1® Magazine: "Can Rain Be Dangerous?" from *Current Health 1®* Magazine, November 1991. Text copyright © 1991 by Weekly Reader Corporation. Published by Weekly Reader Corporation.

Dial Books for Young Readers, a division of Penguin Books USA Inc.: Cover illustration from *Bridges* by Ken Robbins. Copyright © 1991 by Ken Robbins.

Doubleday, a division of Bantam Doubleday Dell Publishing Group, Inc.: Cover illustration from *Why Can't I Fly?* by Ken Brown. Copyright © 1990 by Ken Brown.

Dutton Children's Books, a division of Penguin Books USA Inc.: From *It's an Armadillo!* by Bianca Lavies. Copyright © 1989 by Bianca Lavies.

Farrar, Straus & Giroux, Inc.: "Ribbons of Wind" from *Balloons and Other Poems* by Deborah Chandra. Text copyright © 1988, 1990 by Deborah Chandra.

Frank Fretz: Illustration by Frank Fretz from "Only the Tough Survive" by James Halfpenny in *Ranger Rick* Magazine, December 1993.

Harcourt Brace & Company: Cover illustration from *A River Ran Wild* by Lynne Cherry. Copyright © 1992 by Lynne Cherry.

The Hokuseido Press, Tokyo, Japan: Untitled haiku (Retitled: "Japanese Poem") by Buson from *Haiku*, Vols. 1-4, translated by R. H. Blyth.

Holiday House, Inc.: Cover illustration from *Weather Words and What They Mean* by Gail Gibbons. Copyright © 1990 by Gail Gibbons.

Richard Lewis: Untitled poem (Retitled: "African Bushman Poem") from *Out of the Earth I Sing*, edited by Richard Lewis. Text copyright © 1968 by Richard Lewis.

Little, Brown and Company: From *Four Corners of the Sky: Poems, Chants and Oratory* (Retitled: "Native American Kiowa Verse"), selected by Theodore Clymer. Text copyright © 1975 by Theodore Clymer.

Little, Brown and Company, in Association with Arcade Publishing, Inc.: Cover illustration by Ted Rand from *Water's Way* by Lisa Westberg Peters. Illustration copyright © 1991 by Ted Rand.

Lothrop, Lee & Shepard Books, a division of William Morrow & Company, Inc.: Cover illustration by Catherine Stock from *Galimoto* by Karen Lynn Williams. Illustration copyright © 1990 by Catherine Stock.

National Wildlife Federation: "Amazing Jumping Machine" by Carolyn Duckworth from *Ranger Rick* Magazine, March 1991. Text copyright 1991 by the National Wildlife Federation. "Only the Tough Survive" by James Halfpenny from *Ranger Rick* Magazine, December 1993. Text copyright 1993 by the National Wildlife Federation. Drawings by Jack Shepherd from "Magic Jumpson" in *Ranger Rick* Magazine, March 1991. Copyright 1991 by the National Wildlife Federation.

North-South Books Inc., New York: Cover illustration from *The Air Around Us* by Eleonore Schmid. Copyright © 1992 by Nord-Sud Verlag AG, Gossau Zürich, Switzerland.

Marian Reiner: Untitled haiku (Retitled: "Japanese Poem") by Asayasu from *More Cricket Songs*, translated by Harry Behn. Text copyright © 1971 by Harry Behn.

Sierra Club Books for Children: From *Come Back, Salmon* by Molly Cone. Text copyright © 1992 by Molly Cone.

Simon & Schuster Books for Young Readers, New York: Cover illustration from *Frog Odyssey* by Juliet and Charles Snape. © 1991 by Juliet and Charles Snape.

Gareth Stevens, Inc., Milwaukee, WI: From *Rockets, Probes, and Satellites* by Isaac Asimov. © 1988 by Nightfall, Inc.

Walker and Company: Cover illustration by Valerie A. Kells from *One Earth, a Multitude of Creatures* by Peter and Connie Roop. Illustration copyright © 1992 by Valerie A. Kells.

PHOTO CREDITS
Key: (t)top, (b)bottom, (l)left, (r)right, (c)center, (bg)background.

Front Cover, All Other Photographs: (tl), Robert Maier/Animals Animals; (tr), NASA/International Stock Photo; (c), Jean-Francois Causse/Tony Stone Images; (cr), Kristian Hilsen/Tony Stone Images; (bl), Benn Mitchell/The Image Bank; (br), E.R. Degginger/Color-Pic.
Back Cover, Harcourt Brace & Company Photographs: (t), Greg Leary; (bl), Earl Kogler.
Back Cover, All Other Photographs: (br), Kaz Mori/The Image Bank.
To The Student, Harcourt Brace & Company Photographs: vi(tr), vi(c), Weronica Ankarorn; vi(b), Maria Paraskevas; viii, Earl Kogler; xv(b), Jerry White.
To The Student, All Other Photographs: iv(tl), Neena Wilmot/Stock/Art Images; iv(tr), Jane Burton/Bruce Coleman, Inc.; iv(bl), Dwight R. Kuhn; iv(br), Dave B. Fleetham/Tom Stack & Assoc.; v(t), Dave Bartruff; v(b), Photri; vi(tl), W. Hille/Leo de Wys, Inc.; vii(l), Stephen Dalton/Photo Researchers; vii(r), John Gerlach/Tom Stack & Assoc.; x, David Young-Wolff/PhotoEdit; xi(t), T. Rosenthal/SuperStock; xi(b), Gabe Palmer/The Stock Market; xii, Myrleen Ferguson Cate/PhotoEdit; xiii, Tony Freeman/PhotoEdit; xiv(l), Jeff Greenberg/Photo Researchers; xiv(r), Russell D. Curtis/Photo Researchers; xv(t), Bob Daemmrich; xvi(l), Myrleen Ferguson Cate/PhotoEdit; xvi(r), Bob Daemmrich/Stock, Boston.
Unit A, Harcourt Brace & Company Photographs: A4-A5, A6(t), A7, Dick Krueger; A8, A9, Weronica Ankarorn; A10-A11, Dick Krueger; A16(r), A17(tr), A17(b), A19, A20(b), A22, A27, A37, A38, A43(l), A44, Earl Kogler; A63, Eric Camden; A76, A86, Earl Kogler; A92-A93(bg), David Lavine; A92(t), A93, Earl Kogler.
Unit A, All Other Photographs: Unit Page Divider, Erwin & Peggy Bauer; A1, A2-A3, Alan & Sandy Carey; A3, Hugh P. Smith, Jr.; A6(b), Alan Briere/SuperStock; A12(bg), Index Stock; A12(t), David R. Frazier; A12(b), William Johnson/Stock, Boston; A13(t), Henry Ausloos/Animals Animals; A13(b), Antoinette

Jongen/SuperStock; A14(t), John Cancalosi/Stock, Boston; A14(b), M. Bruce/SuperStock; A15(t), Stephen G. Maka/Lightwave; A15(b), H. Lanks/SuperStock; A16(l), G. Corbett/SuperStock; A17(tl), Stephen J. Krasemann/NHPA; A20(t), M. Burgess/SuperStock; A21, A. Mercieca/SuperStock; A23(t), Dwight R. Kuhn; A23(b), James T. Jones/David R. Frazier Photolibrary; A24(t), SuperStock; A24(b), Stephen G. Maka/Lightwave; A25(t), Gary Bell/The Wildlife Collection; A25(cl), Larry A. Brazil; A25(cr), Stephen J. Krasemann/Valan Photos; A25(b), David Cavagnaro/Peter Arnold, Inc.; A28, The Granger Collection; A30(tl), A. Kaiser/SuperStock; A30(tr), Stephen Dalton/NHPA; A30(b), Aaron Haupt/David R. Frazier Photolibrary; A31, A32(t), SuperStock; A32(c), John Giustina/The Wildlife Collection; A32(b), Sven-Olaf Lindblad/Photo Researchers; A33(t), A33(b), A34(t), A34(c), A34(b), A35(l), A35(r), Bianca Lavies; A36(bg), Rod Planck/Tony Stone Images; A36(t), Scot Stewart; A36(b), Stephen G. Maka/Lightwave; A39(tl), Bill Tronca/Tom Stack & Assoc.; A39(tc), A39(tr), T. Wolf Bolz/TexStockPhotoInc.; A39(bl), David M. Dennis/Tom Stack & Assoc.; A39(bc), Claudio Ferer/Devaney Stock Photos; A39(br) Gerald & Buff Corsi/Tom Stack & Assoc.; A40, Leonard Lee Rue III/Animals Animals; A41, Tetsu Yamazaki; A42, Bob Daemmrich/The Image Works; A43(r), Don Enger/Animals Animals; A45(l), Ron & Valerie Taylor/Bruce Coleman, Inc.; A45(r), A46(t), Zig Leszczynski/Animals Animals; A46(cl), E.R. Degginger/Color-Pic; A46(cr), Renee Lynn/Photo Researchers; A46(b), Holton Collection/SuperStock; A47(tl), Alan G. Nelson/Animals Animals; A47(tr), E.R. Degginger/Animals Animals; A47(c), Fred Whitehead/Animals Animals; A47(b), Dominique Braud/Tom Stack & Assoc.; A48(t), Brian Parker/Tom Stack & Assoc.; A48(b), Oxford Scientific Films/Animals Animals; A49(tl), Dwight R. Kuhn; A49(tc), Lester V. Bergman & Assoc.; A49(tr), Rod Planck/Tom Stack & Assoc.; A49(cl), Biophoto Associates/Photo Researchers; A49(cr), John Shaw/Tom Stack & Assoc.; A49(b), Dave B. Fleetham/Tom Stack & Assoc.; A52(bg), Tim Fitzharris/Masterfile; A52(t) H. Morton/SuperStock; A52(b), John Cancalosi/Valan Photos; A53, D. Robert Franz/The Wildlife Collection; A54(tl), Stephen G. Maka/Lightwave; A54(tr), Hank Andrews/Visuals Unlimited; A54(b), Mike Bacon/Tom Stack & Assoc.; A55(t), Stephen G. Maka/Lightwave; A55(b), SuperStock; A56(t), Stephen G. Maka/Lightwave; A56(c), Gerald & Buff Corsi/Tom Stack & Assoc.; A56(b), Fred Bruemmer/Valan Photos; A57(t), Scot Stewart; A57(b), Western History Department/Denver Public Library; A58(tl), A58(tr), Daniel W. Gotshall; A58(bl) SuperStock; A58(br), Dwight R. Kuhn; A59(t), SuperStock; A59(b), John Cancalosi/Valan Photos; A61(t), M. Bruce/SuperStock; A61(b), SuperStock; A62-A63(bg), Index Stock; A64(t) A64(b) Master's Studio; A65, Jane Burton/Bruce Coleman, Inc.; A66, Mark Sherman/Bruce Coleman, Inc.; A67, Michael S. Quinton; A68(t), Erwin & Peggy Bauer; A68(bl), Frank Fretz; A68(br), Erwin & Peggy Bauer; A69, Stephen J. Krasemann/DRK; A70, Leonard Lee Rue III; A71, Erwin & Peggy Bauer; A72(bg), Gregory Dimijian/Photo Researchers; A72(t), John Colwell/Grant Heilman Photography; A72(b), H. Mark Weidman; A73, David R. Frazier; A74(t), Allen Russell/ProFiles West; A74(c), Doug Perrine/Innerspace Visions; A74(b), John Cancalosi/Tom Stack & Assoc.; A75(t), John Fowler/Valan Photos; A75(cl), Dwight R. Kuhn; A75(cr), Stephen G. Maka/Lightwave; A75(b), Martin Harvey/The Wildlife Collection; A77, Wolfgang Kaehler; A78(t), Dr. Paul V. Loiselle; A78(b), John T. Pennington/Ivy Images; A79, Martin Harvey/The Wildlife Collection; A80, A81(t), A81(b), A82(t), A82(cl), A82(cr), A82(b), A83(t), Dwight R. Kuhn; A83(bl), A83(br), Renee Stockdale/Animals Animals; A84(tl), Dwight R. Kuhn; A84(tr), Tom & Pat Leeson/DRK; A84(bl), Mella

Panzella/Animals Animals; A84(br), Neena Wilmot/Stock/Art Images; A85(tl), Gary Braasch; A85(tr), Brian Parker/Tom Stack & Assoc.; A85(cl), A85(c), SuperStock; A85(cr), Gary Braasch; A85(b), A88(t), A88(cl), A88(cr), A88(b), A89(l), A89(r), Dwight R. Kuhn; A90-A91, Index Stock; A91(l), SuperStock; A91(r), A. Briere/SuperStock; A92(b), Allen Russell/ProFiles West; A94(t), Sven-Olaf Lindblad/Photo Researchers; A94(c), Anthony J. Bond/Valan Photos; A94(b), Stephen J. Krasemann/Valan Photos; A95(l), Wolfgang Bayer/Bruce Coleman, Inc.; A95(r), A. Mercieca/SuperStock.

Unit B, Harcourt Brace & Company Photographs: B4-B5, B6(t), B7(t), B7(b), Dick Krueger; B8, B9, Weronica Ankarorn; B10-B11, Maria Paraskevas; B14, B15, B16, B17, B20, Earl Kogler; B23(cb), Rodney Jones; B28(bc), B29(t), B29(b), B30, B36, B37, Earl Kogler; B40(bg), David Phillips; B41, B42, Earl Kogler; B43, Richard Nowitz; B44, B46(t), B46(b), B47, B53, Earl Kogler; B55(t), B55(b), B56(l), B56(r), B57, Jerry Heasley; B61, B63, B68, Richard T. Nowitz; B76(t), B76(b), Earl Kogler; B77(b), Richard T. Nowitz; 79(t), Earl Kogler.

Unit B, All Other Photographs: Unit Page Divider, A. Farquhar/Valan Photos; B1, Amy Drutman; B2-3, Gordon Wiltsie/Peter Arnold, Inc.; B3, Alan & Sandy Carey; B6(c), R. Dahlquist/SuperStock; B6(b), George Cargill/Lightwave; B12(bg), Jay Maisel; B12, Scott Barrow; B18(l), B18(r), B19(l), B19(r), E.R. Degginger/Bruce Coleman, Inc.; B22(t), SuperStock; B22(ct), David R. Frazier; B22(cb), Scott Barrow; B22(b), Hans & Judy Beste/Earth Scenes; B23(t), Scott Barrow; B23(ct), Harry M. Walker; B23(b), Loren McIntyre; B24(tl), Will & Deni McIntyre/AllStock; B24(t), Tony Freeman/PhotoEdit; B24(cl), J.C. Carton/Bruce Coleman, Inc.; B24(cr), Richard T. Nowitz; B24(b), Fotoconcept; B25(t), John Eastcott, Yva Momatiuk/Valan Photos; B25(b), Sovfoto; B27, David Falconer/David R. Frazier Photolibrary; B28(bg), Dwight R. Kuhn; B28(t), Steve Solum/Bruce Coleman, Inc.; B28(bl), David R. Frazier; B28(br), Dave Bartruff; B32-B33, Gary Black/Masterfile; B32, Peter Griffith/Masterfile; B33, Mark Tomalty/Masterfile; B34, Peter Miller/Photo Researchers; B35(t), Alan Hicks/AllStock; B35(c), Wouterloot-Gregoire/Valan Photos; B35(b), Joyce Photographics/Valan Photos; B36-B37(bg), Dick Thomas/Visuals Unlimited; B40(t), Phil Degginger/Color-Pic; B40(b), Tony Freeman/PhotoEdit; B48, The Granger Collection; B50(bg), John Running/Stock, Boston; B50, The Granger Collection; B51(t) David R. Frazier; B51(b), Photri; B52, Runk, Schoenberger/Grant Heilman Photography; B54(l), A. Farquhar/Valan Photos; B54(r), SuperStock; B58(bg), David Woodfall/Tony Stone Images; B58(t), E.R. Degginger/Color-Pic; B58(b), Jose L. Pelaez/The Stock Market; B59, R. Llewellyn/SuperStock; B60(t), E.R. Degginger/Color-Pic; B60(c), Tony Freeman/PhotoEdit; B60(b), Anna Zuckerman/PhotoEdit; B62-B63(bg), E.R. Degginger/Color-Pic; B64, B65, B66, David R. Frazier; B67, Tony Freeman/PhotoEdit; B69, Ruth Dixon; B70, North Wind; B71, Phil Degginger/Color-Pic; B72(t), Bill Weedmark; B72(b), Dave Bartruff; B73, Grapes Michaud/Photo Researchers; B74-B75, J.R. Page/Valan Photos; B75(t), Valerie Wilkinson/Valan Photos; B75(b), SuperStock; B76-B77(bg), Greg Vaughn/Tom Stack & Assoc.; B77(t), Aaron Haupt/David R. Frazier Photolibrary; B78(t), Runk, Schoenberger/Grant Heilman Photography; B78(b), Mark Tomalty/Masterfile; B79(c) Gary Black/Masterfile; B79(b), John Heseltine/Photo Researchers; B80(l), Peter Griffith/Masterfile; B80(r), A. Upitis/SuperStock.

Unit C, Harcourt Brace & Company Photographs: C4-C5, C6(c), C6(b), C7(t), David Phillips; C7(c), Earl Kogler; C7(b), David Phillips; C8, C9, Weronica Ankarorn; C10-C11, C13, C14(b), C15(t), C15(bl), C15(br), C16, C17, C19(tl), C19(tr), C19(b), Earl Kogler; C20-C21(bg), Jerry White; C20, C21(t), C21(bl), C21(br),

C22(tr), C22(br), C23(tl), C23(c), C23(b), C24, C25, C28(l), C28(c), C28(r), C29(t), C29(b), Earl Kogler; C32(t), Gerald Ratto; C35, Earl Kogler; C36, C37, C39, C40, C43(t), C43(c), C43(b), C45(t), Dick Krueger; C45(b), Rob Downey; C46-C47(bg), Dick Krueger; C46, C47, Weronica Ankarorn; C48, Dick Krueger; C52(b), C53, Maria Paraskevas; C54(t), Bruce Wilson; C54(cl), Weronica Ankarorn; C54(cr), Earl Kogler; C54(b), Weronica Ankarorn; C55, Earl Kogler; C56(t), C56(b), C57(t), Maria Paraskevas; C58, Earl Kogler; C59(t), C59(b), Maria Paraskevas; C60, C61, C63(t), C63(b), C64, Earl Kogler; C66(t), C66(b), C67, Robert Landau; C73, C75(t), Earl Kogler; C75(b), David Phillips; C76(t), Earl Kogler; C76(b), David Phillips; C77, Jerry White; C78(l), Earl Kogler; C79(tl), Bruce Wilson; C79(tr), Earl Kogler; C79(bl), David Phillips; C79(br), Earl Kogler.

Unit C, All Other Photographs: Unit Page Divider, Bud Nielsen/Li htwave; C1, Richard T. Nowitz/Valan Photos; C2-C3, David R. Frazier; C3, Rapho/Photo Researchers; C6(t), SuperStock; C12(bg), Harold Sund/The Image Bank; C12(t), James Blank/Zephyr Pictures; C12(b), W. Hille/Leo de Wys, Inc.; C14(t), Terry Wild Studio; C14(c), Ewing Galloway; C22(l), T. Matsumoto/Sygma; C23(tr), E.R. Degginger/Earth Scenes; C24-C25(bg), NASA; C26, The Bettmann Archive; C27, Lewis Portnoy/Spectra-Action; C30, Christopher Liu/ChinaStock; C31(t), Milt & Joan Mann/Cameramann; C31(b), Harry M. Walker; C32(b), Robert Frerck/Odyssey Productions; C33, Yves Tessier/Tessima; C34(bg), Roy Ooms/Masterfile; C34(l), John Terence Turner/FPG; C34(b), Alissa Crandall; C38-C39(bg), SuperStock; C41, Paul Souders/AllStock; C42(t), David R. Frazier; C42(c), C42(b), Alan & Sandy Carey; C44, NASA/Photri; C49, Dave Bartruff; C50-C51(bg), William Warren/West Light; C50(all), C51(all), Insurance Institute for Highway Safety; C52(bg), Index Stock; C52(t), Bud Nielsen/Lightwave; C57(b), Neena M. Wilmot/Stock/Art Images; C62(t), Ruth Dixon; C62(c), Dave Bartruff; C62(b), Aldo Mastrocola/Lightwave; C68, Steinman, Boynton, Gronquist & Birdsall; C70-C71, Frederic Stein/FPG; C72-C73(bg), Ken Graham; C74-C75(bg), SuperStock; C76-C77(bg), Andrew Sacks/Tony Stone Images; C78(r), Lewis Portony/Spectra-Action.

Unit D, Harcourt Brace & Company Photographs: D4-D5, Earl Kogler; D6(t), Dick Krueger; D8, D9, Weronica Ankarorn; D10-D11, D22, D23(b), Britt Runion; D24, Earl Kogler; D25, D26-D27, Britt Runion; D37(t), D37(b), D60(t), D62(t), D62(b) D63, D64, D65, Earl Kogler; D72, D73, Robert Landau; D76, D77(t), Richard T. Nowitz; D77(b), Earl Kogler.

Unit D, All Other Photographs: Unit Page Divider, Mark J. Thomas/Dembinsky Photo Assoc; D1, D2-D3, Larry Lefever/Grant Heilman Photography; D3, Adam Jones/Dembinsky Photo Assoc.; D6(b), William McKinney/FPG; D7, Neena M. Wilmot/Stock/Art Images; D12(bg), Greg Nikas/Viesti Assoc.; D12(t), David R. Frazier; D12(b), Ruth Dixon; D13, Rod Planck/Tom Stack & Assoc.; D14(t), M.P.L. Fogden/Bruce Coleman, Inc.; D14(b), E.R. Degginger/Bruce Coleman, Inc.; D15(t), S. Maimone/SuperStock; D15(b), John Gerlach/Tom Stack & Assoc.; D16-D17(bg), Gabe Palmer/The Stock Market; D16, Gary Meszaros/Dembinsky Photo Assoc.; D17, John Shaw/Bruce Coleman, Inc.; D18(t), Mark J. Thomas/Dembinsky Photo Assoc.; D18(b), J.H. Robinson/Photo Researchers; D19, Gay Bumgarner/Photo Network; D23(t), Patti Murray/Earth Scenes; D28-D29, Betsy Blass/Photo Researchers; D29(tl), Karl H. Switak/Photo Researchers; D29(tr), E.R. Degginger/Color-Pic; D30(bg), Stephen G. Maka/Lightwave; D30(t), Stephen Dalton/Photo Researchers; D30(b), Stephen J. Krasemann/Valan Photos; D31, Stephen Dalton/Photo Researchers; D32(t), Zig Leszczynski/Animals Animals; D32(c), J.H. Robinson/Animals Animals; D32(b), Zig Leszczynski/Animals Animals; D33(t), Kim Taylor/Bruce Coleman, Inc.; D33(b), Gregory Dimijian/Photo Researchers; D38(t), D38(b), D39(t), D39(c), D39(b), Dwight R. Kuhn; D44(bg), SuperStock; D44(t), P. Van Rhijn/SuperStock; D44(b), Bob & Clara Calhoun/Bruce Coleman, Inc.; D46, D47 Dwight R. Kuhn; D48(t), Mildred McPhee/Valan Photos; D48(cl), Bill Beatty/Wild & Natural; D48(cr), E.R. Degginger/Color-Pic; D48(cb), Glen D. Chambers; D48(bl), J. Faircloth/Transparencies; D48(br), Oxford Scientific Films/Animals Animals; D49(t), J.A. Wilkinson/Valan Photos; D49(cl), Bill Beatty/Wild & Natural; D49(cr), Steve Maslowski/Valan Photos; D49(cb), Thomas Kitchin/Tom Stack & Assoc.; D49((bl), Bill Beatty/Wild & Natural; D49(br), John Shaw/Bruce Coleman, Inc.; D54, Phillip Norton/Valan Photos; D56-D57, Manley/SuperStock; D56, John Eastcott, Yva Momatiuk/Stock, Boston; D58(bg), R. Dahlquist/SuperStock; D58(t), M. Roessler/SuperStock; D58(b), D59, SuperStock; D60(b), Mark E. Gibson; D61(t), Dwight R. Kuhn; D61(b), A. Hennek/SuperStock; D66, D67(t), D67(b), D68, D69, D70(tl), D70(tr), D70(b), Sidnee Wheelwright; D71(t), Chris Huss/The Wildlife Collection; D71(c), D71(b), Sidnee Wheelwright; D74-D75(bg), SuperStock; D75, Nancy Sefton/Photo Researchers; D76-D77(bg), Andy Caulfield/The Image Bank; D78, James H. Carmichael, Jr./The Image Bank.

Unit E, Harcourt Brace & Company Photographs: E4-E5, Weronica Ankarorn; E6(t), Earl Kogler; E6(b), Dick Krueger; E8, E9, Weronica Ankarorn; E10-E11, E13, E14(t), E14(b), E15, Earl Kogler; E16, Weronica Ankarorn; E17, E20, E23, E24, E27, E29, E30, E38(t), E41(t), E41(b), E50, E57, E61, Earl Kogler; E91(r), Dick Krueger; E92(t), Earl Kogler; E92(b), Maria Paraskevas; E93, Dick Krueger.

Unit E, All Other Photographs: Unit Page Divider, Frank P. Rossotto/The Stock Market; E1, E2-E3, Neena M. Wilmot/Stock/Art Images; E2, Archiv/Photo Researchers; E3, Frank P. Rossotto/The Stock Market; E7, Milt & Joan Mann/Cameramann; E12(bg), Craig Aurness/West Light; E12(t), Allen S. Stone/Devaney Stock Photos; E12(b), Kennon Cooke/Valan Photos; E21, Wide World Photos; E26(bg), M. Stephenson/West Light; E26(t), K. Sklute/SuperStock; E26(b) North Wind; E30-E31(bg), Alese & Mort Pechter/The Stock Market; E33, Ron Watts/Black Star; E35, Linc Cornell/Light Sources; E38(bg), J.A. Kraulis/Masterfile; E38(b), Norman Owen Tomalin/Bruce Coleman, Inc.; E40(t), Russ Kinne/Comstock; E40(b), Spencer Swanger/Tom Stack & Assoc.; E47, William Carter/Photo Researchers; E54(bg), Paul Chesley/Tony Stone Images; E54(t), Steve Kaufman/Ken Graham Agency; E54(b), UPI/Bettmann; E55(tl), Percy Jones/Archive Photos; E55(tr), Photri; E55(c), Charles Palek/Tom Stack & Assoc.; E55(bl), Photri; E55(br), Frank P. Rossotto/Tom Stack & Assoc.; E60(l), Richard P. Smith/Tom Stack & Assoc.; E60(r), Ken Gouvin/Comstock; E62, Gerald & Buff Corsi/Tom Stack & Assoc.; E63(t), Gary Benson/Comstock; E63(b), John McDermott/Tony Stone Images; E64(t), Neena M. Wilmot/Stock/Art Images; E64(b), John Shaw/Tom Stack & Assoc.; E65, Bruce Matheson/PHOTO/NATS; E66, Archive Photos; E67, UPI/Bettmann Newsphotos; E68, The Bettmann Archive; E70, E71, U.S. Air Force; E72(bg), NASA; E72(t), NASA/Photri; E72(b), E78, NASA; E79, J. Novak/SuperStock; E80(t), Hank Brandli and Rob Downey; E80(b), European Space Agency/Photo Researchers; E81, David R. Frazier; E82, NASA/Photri; E84, E86(t), E86(c), NASA; E86(b), E87(t), Frank P. Rossotto/Tom Stack & Assoc.; E87(c), NASA; E87(b), W. Kaufmann/Photo Researchers; E88(tl), NASA; E88(tr), E88(c), E88(bl), E88(br), NASA/Photri; E89(t), NASA; E89(b), NASA/Photri; E90-E91(bg), Wendy Shattil, Bob Rozinski/Tom Stack & Assoc.; E91(l), NASA; E92-E93(bg), Greg Vaughn/Tom Stack & Assoc.; E94, Gerald & Buff Corsi/Tom Stack & Assoc.; E95, NASA.